The Study of Religion in Canada/
Sciences Religieuses au Canada : 5

The Study of Religion in Canada /
Sciences Religieuses au Canada

The Study of Religion in Canada/Sciences Religieuses au Canada is a series of publications planned as "A State-of-the-Art Review" of religious studies in Canada. Each volume in the series covers a particular geographic region. The aim is to present a descriptive and analytical study of courses, programs and research currently being undertaken in the field of religious studies in Canada. The descriptive aspect of the study takes into account the history, nature and rationale of courses and programs, and statistics concerning enrolments and faculty involved. The analytical aspect of the study is concerned with trends and directions of programs, both projected and actual, the relationship of programs and courses to the training and research of faculty, the appeal of courses and programs, and the relevance of such courses and programs to larger issues in society.

To date there has been no thorough study of the state of the art of religious studies in Canada. Information concerning religious studies has been confined basically to university and college catalogues and course information in guidance counselling offices in high schools. The descriptive and analytical aspects of this study serve to provide valuable information generally not contained in lists of courses, and will aid students, counsellors, and educators in both public and private institutions.

This study, the research it has involved and the publication of its results, was made possible by a generous grant from the Social Sciences and Humanities Research Council of Canada.

THE STUDY OF RELIGION IN CANADA

Volume 5

The Study of Religion in British Columbia: A State-of-the-Art Review

Brian J. Fraser

Published for the Canadian Corporation for Studies in Religion/Corporation Canadienne des Sciences Religieuses by Wilfrid Laurier University Press

1995

Canadian Cataloguing in Publication Data

Fraser, Brian J. (Brian John), 1947-
  The study of religion in British Columbia

(The study of religion in Canada = Sciences
religieuses au Canada ; 5)
Includes index.
ISBN 0-88920-261-3

1. Religion – Study and teaching (Higher) –
British Columbia.   2. Theology – Study and teaching
(Higher) – British Columbia.   I. Canadian
Corporation for Studies in Religion.   II. Title.
III. Series: The study of religion in Canada ; 5.

BL41.F73 1995   200'.71'1711   C95-931990-5

Cover design by Michael Baldwin, MSIAD

Printed in Canada

The Study of Religion in British Columbia: A State-of-the-Art Review has
been produced from a manuscript supplied in electronic form by the author.

Order from:
WILFRID LAURIER UNIVERSITY PRESS
Waterloo, Ontario, Canada   N2L 3C5

Contents

Preface[*]

Religion has been an integral part of life in the regions of North America now known as British Columbia since the first human settlements some ten thousand years ago. The study of religion at the post-secondary level of our modern educational system, however, is less than one hundred years old. This book seeks to chronicle the development of the institutions of higher education in which religion has been and is the primary subject of study and to describe the methods that have been and are being used to understand the religious dimension of human endeavour.

The institutions in which the study of religion has taken place have changed substantially over the last century, especially since the 1960s. During these past thirty years, institutions established earlier have altered in character and new players have entered the field. At present, seven institutions offer degree programs in the study of religion and one university has a major research centre in the field. The University of British Columbia is a public comprehensive university with a department offering undergraduate and graduate degrees in religious studies. Trinity Western University is a private comprehensive university with a department offering undergraduate degrees in theological studies. Vancouver School of Theology is a mainline Protestant seminary offering graduate degrees in theology. Regent College is a conservative evangelical Protestant graduate school of theology. The Associated Canadian Theological

---

[*] The notes to the Preface are on p. x.

vii

Schools, a consortium of small colleges representing the believers' church tradition of conservative evangelical Protestantism, offers graduate degrees in theology. Christ the King Seminary is operated by the Benedictine Order in the Roman Catholic tradition and offers undergraduate and graduate degrees. Columbia Bible College is a Mennonite school offering degrees in theology. Western Pentecostal Bible College is the theological college for the British Columbia District of the Pentecostal Assemblies of Canada and offers an undergraduate degree in theology. The University of Victoria established the Centre for Studies in Religion and Society in 1991 to encourage the study of religion in relation to a wide range of scientific and cultural disciplines.[1]

Two basic approaches, which may be classified as religious studies and theological studies, characterize the study of religion in these institutions in British Columbia. As used in this survey, religious studies refers to a scholarly neutral and non-advocative field of study that is characterized by rigour and detachment in its approach, by a variety of methodologies drawn from the humanities and the social sciences in its research, and by results that intend to elucidate the questions of human existence that religions have always tried to confront. It is conducted in a public and pluralistic institution. The University of British Columbia is the only one that offers a program in religious studies. The other institutions are engaged in various kinds of theological studies for professional, confessional, proselytizing, and/or apologetic purposes. Theological studies, on the other hand, refers to a scholarly committed and advocative field of study that is characterized by self-critical engagement in its approach, by a variety of methodologies in its research, and by results that intend to enhance participation in and contribution to the religious traditions and communities that govern the institutions in which the study takes place.[2]

In the other volumes in the Canadian Corporation for the Study of Religion (CCSR) series on the study of religion in Canada, the focus has been on religious studies in the secular university, with minimal attention being paid to various approaches of theological studies. Indeed, the titles of the volumes have clearly indicated that their subject is the field of religious studies. Partly because of the nature of the study of religion in British Columbia, and partly because of my own vocational base in theological studies, I have chosen to focus on the broader subject indicated by the original designation of the series as a whole, i.e., the study of religion. A comprehensive, state-of-the-art review of the study of religion in British Columbia, as the series title promises, requires that appropriate attention be paid to both religious studies and theological studies.

Some of the centres in which the study of religion at the post-secondary level are being pursued in British Columbia have been studied previously, but none of them has been seen as part of a larger whole. It is the purpose of this study, therefore, to examine all the approaches to the study of religion taken by these institutions and draw some conclusions concerning their interrelations.

The latest census figures indicate that the religious composition of the present population (2,713,615) consists of two main groups. The largest group, representing three-quarters of the population, identifies itself as Christian (2,011,280). The other significant group, representing about one-fifth of the population, identifies itself as having no religious preference (566,905). The dominance of the Christian majority is not surprising given the immigration patterns which have been in place until recently. It is striking, however, that British Columbia is the only province in Canada where Roman Catholics are a minority (526,355) and the Protestants constitute a very sizeable majority (1,484,925). The Protestant majority, however, is divided into two parties: the mainline or broad church denominations (1,234,925) and the conservative or evangelical churches (250,000). Though this division is commonly used and generally valid, it must be noted that many Christians who identify themselves as conservative or evangelical remain attached to the mainline denominations. Census figures, of course, do not bear any relationship to the number of individuals who are actually members of churches nor to the number found in church on Sundays. But they do indicate how people identify themselves and their group within this society. Furthermore, the census figures provide some information on the size of the groups supporting the various types of educational institutions to be found in the province.

This review of the study of religion in British Columbia adopts a historical approach. It chronicles the development of the various institutions that pursue the study of religion at the post-secondary level in the province from their beginnings until 1992, identifies the constituencies that established and supported them, explores how the internal dynamics of the institutions and their faculties shaped their approaches to the study of religion, and analyzes their interrelationships. The first chapter examines the formative stages of the institutions. Chapter two focuses on the programs and curriculum developed in these institutions. In the third chapter, the scholars who have taught and researched in these institutions are considered. A concluding section seeks to provide a critical analysis of the current state of the study of religion in British Columbia.

The study itself has had a long and melancholy history. It was begun by Chuck Anderson, with the help of Linda Christensen. By the fall of 1989, Chuck's health made it impossible for him to continue the project and he asked Keith Clifford to take it over. In February of 1990, Keith died suddenly of a heart attack with much of the research data collected but the manuscript only half finished. I agreed to revise and complete it. I have followed Keith's design for the book and used many of the interpretive frameworks he suggested. Harold Coward, the general editor of the series, deserves special thanks for his persistent patience. The manuscript has been reviewed thoroughly by Don Lewis, Joe Richardson, Harold Coward, Bob Stewart, and Tirthankar Bose. Each made insightful suggestions that I have attempted to incorporate into the manuscript to strengthen its clarity and thoroughness. I have not done everything they suggested and bear full responsibility for the remaining faults.

Notes

1 The characterizations of these institutions is based on a list of 11 institutional types developed in Ray L. Hart, "Religious and Theological Studies in American Higher Education: A Pilot Study," *Journal of the American Academy of Religion,* 59, 4 (Winter 1991): 715-92.

2 For a survey of perceptions on the distinctions between religious studies and theological studies, see Hart, "Pilot Study," 730-44. Hart notes that this is a major problem in the study of religion and identifies four questions that emerge in attempts to resolve it: what is being studied, who is studying it, where is it being studied, and what is the audience of the study. The responses reported by Hart and his colleagues show little consensus. For a survey of the Canadian discussion, especially in Ontario, see Harold Remus, William Closson James, and Daniel Fraikin, *Religious Studies in Ontario: A State-of-the-Art Review* (Waterloo: Wilfrid Laurier University Press, 1992): 24-34. The Remus, James, and Fraikin study differs from the present one in that it focuses primarily on religious studies. For a review of the development of religious studies in North America, see Harold Remus, "Religion as an Academic Discipline: Origins, Nature, and Changing Understandings," in *Encyclopedia of the American Religious Experience*, vol. 3, ed. Charles H. Lippy and Peter W. Williams (New York: Scribner's, 1988), 1653-64, 1668.

Vancouver, B.C., Spring 1995   Brian J. Fraser

1

Origins and Developments*

The study of religion at the college and university level in British Columbia has been primarily a twentieth-century development. During the first six decades of the century, Christianity was the only religion studied. The approach taken was that of theological studies. Since the 1960s, however, changes in Canada's immigration policy have produced a more racially diverse and religiously pluralistic society in BC. These societal changes have been reflected in the introduction of a different way of studying religion at the university level over the past thirty years in the Department of Religious Studies at UBC. Judaism, Islam, Buddhism, and Hinduism, along with Christianity, have been studied in the department from a more objective and non-partisan perspective. The study of Christianity remains predominant in the province, however, especially because of the new institutions of Christian theological studies established since the 1960s.

An examination of the origins and development of the various post-secondary institutions that pursued the study of religion in BC is, therefore, an appropriate place to begin, as it provides a framework for viewing the changes that have taken place in the past and establishes a context for studying the problems and possibilities that have opened up for the future.

---

* The notes to Chapter 1 are on pp. 32-37.

The Study of Religion in British Columbia
Prior to the 1960s

During the period 1890-1960, the main reason for instituting the study of religion at the college level in BC was to prepare men and women for leadership in the local Christian communities and in the various mission fields of the sponsoring denominations. The first group in the province to found educational institutions for this purpose was Protestant. The Methodists established Columbian College at New Westminster in 1891. It offered some courses in theology, but it was mainly a liberal arts college that its founders hoped would provide the nucleus of a provincial university. With the establishment of Vancouver as the western terminus of the CPR, however, it quickly became apparent that Vancouver rather than New Westminster would become the major metropolis on the West Coast and that it would become the site for a provincial university.

In 1894 an act of the BC legislature permitted the province's high schools to affiliate with Canadian universities. The first university to take advantage of this act was McGill University which, utilizing funds for extension provided by Sir William Macdonald, the Montreal tobacco merchant, sent Dr. Henry Marshall Tory to Vancouver to make affiliation arrangements betweem the Vancouver High School and McGill. In 1899, part of the Vancouver High School was renamed Vancouver College and affiliated with McGill.[1] The first classes leading to McGill degrees began in the fall of 1906.

During the first decade of the twentieth century, BC's population more than doubled. The membership of the Anglican Church in the province almost tripled, while the membership of the Methodist and Presbyterian churches more than doubled. As membership in these denominations grew, it became apparent that an adequate supply of clergy would not come from outside the province. The only way for the churches to provide such leadership, therefore, was to create colleges to train their own ministers. The Presbyterians were the first to respond with the establishment of Westminster Hall in 1907. They were followed by the evangelical Anglicans who set up Latimer Hall in 1910 and by the high church Anglicans who established St. Mark's in 1912.[2] The Methodists also incorporated the theological department of Columbian College as a separate institution called Ryerson College in 1912, but no separate buildings were created for this theological college until after World War I. All of the other Protestant mainline theological colleges were established immediately prior to World War I and all but Ryerson College were located in houses in Vancouver's west end.

All of these schools were struggling institutions inadequately funded and poorly housed. Their libraries were made up largely of books donated by retired ministers; none of their teaching staffs had academic doctorates or post-graduate training in European or American universities. The teachers in these schools were drawn from the ranks of the clergy and in many cases they offered their services on a part-time basis while carrying on their ministerial duties in Vancouver's churches. In all cases the curriculum of these colleges was virtually identical with that offered in the more established theological colleges in eastern Canada. Indeed, all these schools were attempting to duplicate the patterns set by the eastern Canadian schools; Columbian and Ryerson looked to Victoria University in Toronto, while Westminster Hall relied on the Presbyterian experience at Manitoba College in Winnipeg. This college had established a summer school in 1893 that allowed students to pursue their studies in the summer and to return to their mission fields for the rest of the year. Latimer Hall was modelled on Wycliffe College in Toronto, from which it drew most of its staff, and St. Mark's set out to be a copy of Trinity College, Toronto.

Given the financial struggle that each of these small theological institutions laboured under, cutting costs was a major necessity; the most obvious way to do so was through cooperation. The high church and low church communities merged their colleges in the early 1920s to form the Anglican Theological College. The formation of the United Church of Canada in 1925, among the Congregationalists, the Methodists, and two-thirds of the Presbyterians in Canada, brought their colleges into Union College in 1925. In 1927, both Anglican and United institutions moved into adjacent facilities on the new UBC campus in Point Grey. The depression of the 1930s encouraged further cooperation between the two denominations. Agreement on the core curriculum for professional education of their clergy provided the basis. Both colleges placed a high priority on the knowledge of Scripture, and by the 1930s both had adopted similar approaches to the critical study of the Old and New Testaments. Doctrines regarding church, sacraments, and ministry differed, but there was fundamental agreement on the central doctrines of the Incarnation, the Atonement, and the Trinity. The most significant differences were in the area of practical theology. The degree of commonality, however, made it possible to plan cooperatively for faculty appointments from the 1930s through to the 1960s in order to keep costs within manageable limits.[3]

In spite of such careful planning, neither college had the faculty, library, nor financial resources to receive full accreditation from the Association of Theological Schools in the United States and Canada, an international body formed in 1918 to establish standards of excellence by which theological schools could be measured. Studies launched in the 1960s by both the ATS and the Canadian churches concluded that there were too many small colleges in Canada with too few faculty training too few candidates for the ministry. Closures and amalgamations were recommended and implemented.[4] Following several years of study and discussion, the Anglican Theological College and Union College joined together to form the Vancouver School of Theology in 1971. The ATS granted the new school full accreditation in 1975.

For many of those interested in the future of university education in BC, the arrangement with McGill was simply a stopgap measure that would serve the needs of students until such time as arrangements for the establishment of an independent university could be finalized. By December 1910 Dr. Henry Esson Young, the provincial minister of education in the government of Sir Richard McBride, who had been instructed to take action on the university question, had chosen a site for the new university in Point Grey.[5] In November 1912 the Vancouver architects Sharp and Thompson were declared the winners of a design competition for the new university. On 17 February 1913 Dr. Young announced that the first president of UBC would be Dr. Frank Fairchild Wesbrook, a Canadian who had moved from the University of Manitoba Medical School to become a professor, and then dean, of the Medical School at the University of Minnesota.[6]

These early steps toward the establishment of a provincial university in BC alerted the theological colleges to the advantages of a move to the Point Grey site, because all of the early plans for the university contained a site for the theological colleges. Its location in the northeast corner of the campus was referred to as the Theological Square; each college was offered a five-acre parcel of land in this area on a 999-year lease. World War I delayed construction of the university, and it was not until 1925 that classes began on the new site. Thus, the study of religion on the UBC campus commenced in

1927 with two institutions, Union College and the Anglican Theological College, designed for the professional education of clergy.

The buildings of these colleges were among the most beautiful on the campus and, since both schools had 999-year leases on their property, it appeared as if they had built for a millennium. When the depression descended on the province a few years later, some believed that they had overbuilt and, since Union College had a deficit every year but two between 1928 and 1937, which accumulated to $11,147.00 by 1937, there appeared to be some basis for the charge.[7] The lack of students throughout the 1930s and the war years, however, was a more serious problem, and the leadership of the college seems to have been part of the reason for this crisis. Dr. J.G. Brown, who had been on the staff of Ryerson College prior to union, became principal when Union College was founded. From the flood of complaints that reached the United Church's Council on Theological Education concerning Brown's administration of the college and its residences, it appears that he was an extremely difficult person to deal with and, as far as the students were concerned, an unreasonable disciplinarian . On several occasions, representatives from the Board of Education in Toronto were sent out to investigate these complaints. But since Dr. Brown had the support of the college board and they refused to take any action against him, the college continued to be largely ineffective until 1948 when Brown finally retired.[8] Another factor in the situation concerned the other two members of the faculty; Dr. W. H. Smith, who was 71 in 1938, and Dr. Sanford, who was 66, could not retire because adequate provision had not been made for their pensions.

The situation at Union College did not change until 1948 when Dr. W.S. Taylor was appointed principal and two young faculty members were hired: Vernon Fawcett in Old Testament and John Webster Grant in church history.[9] This reversal in the college's fortunes was also assisted by the full support of the university's new president, Dr. Norman Mackenzie, who made his support public in an address to the autumn convocation of Union College in 1948. He said:

A continual and bitter battle is being waged for the minds and souls, the convictions and emotions of youth in our universities. I am determined, so far as lies in my power, that they shall be shown not only the Christian moral and spiritual values, but also Christ Himself. For this reason I set high value on the presence upon the campus of a university with a secular foundation, of theological institutions like Union College and the Anglican College here.[10]

With this type of recognition and support from the university's president, the colleges entered a decade of vigorous growth and cooperation, not only with one another but also with the university.

The growth was sparked both by academic policy changes and by a financial campaign that was launched in 1955 to provide Union College with an endowment fund, for it was the only United Church theological college in Canada without one. The campaign was sufficiently successful to provide funds for a married students' residence and a principal's residence as well as a measure of endowment. Parallel to this financial augmentation was an academic one. Prior to 1957 it was possible for students planning to enter the ministry to get credit towards their arts degrees by taking religious knowledge courses offered by the theological colleges. In 1957, the university approved a new policy in which courses in religion taught by members of the affiliated colleges would be open to all students for credit. The initial impetus for this new policy came neither from the university nor the theological colleges, but from the alumni association. In June 1952 Ormonde Hall, the editor of the *Alumni Chronicle*, published a brief article on "Religion and U.B.C." After noting that publicly supported universities, like UBC, had become almost pagan because of the interpretation of the University Act in BC, he suggested that the University of Iowa could provide an example of how this problem was being handled in the United States.[11] Hall's article caught the attention of several prominent members of the alumni association and they recommended the establishment of a committee under the chairmanship of Dr. W.G. Black to study the "Iowa Plan."[12]

The committee produced an extensive report in 1954 which recommended that six units of credit in religious studies courses taught by professors from the theological colleges should be available to all students in arts and sciences. Dr. MacKenzie recommended that this report should be presented to the Senate at its meeting of 9 February 1955, and after it was approved the Senate set up its own committee on religious studies courses.[13] These courses were carefully screened by the Faculty of Arts and Science and approval was given for a course in church history taught by John W. Grant and a course in Old Testament taught by Vernon Fawcett. The following year, while Grant was on study leave in India, Dr. W. S. Taylor taught the first course on "The Great Religions of the World" to be offered for credit at UBC. While these courses placed extra demands on the college's small staff, they were willingly undertaken as "a contribution to the establishment of a Department of Religious Studies in the university, a project which now seems close to achievement."[14] With rising enrollments and two additional appointments to its faculty, George Tuttle and Reg Wilson, the decade between 1949 and 1959 saw Union College finally achieve the level of efficiency and academic respectability that its founders had envisaged in 1927.[15]

While the depression, World War II, and leadership problems at Union College brought with them many difficulties, the theological colleges had to deal with another serious issue during their first two decades on the university campus. Before the colleges occupied their new buildings, a major split between liberal and conservative factions had occurred within the Protestant community in BC. This split in turn led to the establishment in the lower mainland of an alternative educational institution for conservative Protestants, known as the Vancouver Bible Training College.[16] In 1917, when the Vancouver Ministerial Association refused to sponsor the evangelistic campaign of Dr. French E. Oliver, an ordained Presbyterian minister attached to the Bible Institute of Los Angeles, because of his well-known attacks on modernism, a group of Vancouver businessmen and clergy formed the Vancouver Evangelistic Movement to sponsor him. Shortly thereafter this group listed among its purposes the sponsorship of mass evangelism campaigns, the establishment of a local bible training school, and the provision of a permanent base in the city for the China Inland Mission. It was agreed that when the bible school came into being, Walter Ellis would become its principal. After completing his MA in Semitics at the University of Toronto and his BD at Wycliffe College, and being ordained as an Anglican priest, Ellis had joined the faculty of Bishop Latimer Hall in Vancouver in 1914. In 1917 he became active in the Vancouver Evangelistic Movement. In accepting the principalship of the Vancouver Bible Training College, however, he had no intention of leaving the Anglican Church or his teaching position at Bishop Latimer Hall. But in 1918 A.U. dePencier, the Bishop of New Westminster, fired Ellis from his teaching position and removed his licence to preach in the Anglican Church because of his involvement in an interdenominational school. Ellis, therefore, had no other option but to become the full-time principal of the new bible school. In 1926, in order to supplement his income, Ellis became a Presbyterian minister and was inducted into Fairview Presbyterian Church, a congregation largely made up of former members of Chalmers Presbyterian Church who had refused to enter the United Church of Canada in 1925. In this capacity Ellis represented the two major splits (or two aspects of the same split between liberals and conservatives) that had occurred in the Vancouver Protestant community before the Anglican and United Church colleges opened their doors.

The Vancouver Bible Training School was the second bible college established in Canada.[17] The first was the Toronto Bible College, established in 1894. Ellis was a close friend of Dr. John McNicol, the president of the Toronto Bible College, and the Vancouver school was closely patterned after the Toronto model. Indeed, its curriculum, organizational structure, and doctrinal position were virtually identical with that of Toronto.[18] Its original intention was not to become a training centre for ministers nor to compete with the theological colleges. Its educational requirements were more flexible than those of the seminaries and it never conceived of itself as a post-baccalaureate institution. Consequently, it issued diplomas rather than theological degrees and it never sought degree granting powers. Yet it did become a competitor, because between 1918 and 1953 one hundred and fifty-four of its students entered some form of Christian ministry in a full-time capacity and a large proportion of these went overseas as missionaries. Moreover, funds that might have otherwise gone to the theological colleges were directed to the Vancouver Bible Training College. Thus the split in Protestant ranks affected both the enrollment and funding of the theological colleges.

With its off-campus location and lack of university affiliation reflecting the alienation of the conservative Protestant community from the scientific and secular outlook of UBC, some might think that this institution was of little significance in relation to the modern study of religion at the post-secondary level, especially when its curriculum was largely focused on the nonscientific study of the Bible. But as this school provided the model for many other bible colleges that appeared on the scene following its demise in 1956, its history is essential background for any understanding of some of the more recent developments in the study of religion in BC. Furthermore, the curriculum was not quite as narrow as it might initially have appeared, because Ellis refused to have anything to do with the dispensationalist interpretation of Scripture. Finally, because of the school's close association with the China Inland Mission house in Vancouver, students were continually exposed to missionaries working in the mission fields of China. Granted that Confucianism, Taoism, and Buddhism were viewed as various forms of heathenism that had to be vanquished in the name of the Gospel, students at the Vancouver Bible Training College, at least until the end of World War II, probably knew as much or more about these Chinese religions than their counterparts in the campus-based theological colleges.

While the Anglican and United Churches were the only Protestant denominations to have theological colleges affiliated with UBC during the years 1924 to 1960, Protestants were not the only denominations who were teaching religion at the post-secondary level in the province. The Roman Catholic Church also established institutions during this period. In 1896 a junior seminary was established in New Westminster, but it was closed in 1909 and it was not until October 1931 that the Seminary of Christ the King was established in Ladner. This, however, was a minor seminary that began as a high school. It was not until 1940 that it evolved into an institution which offered a course in philosophy similar to that required for the BA degree. In order to complete the three years of theological training necessary for ordination, students had to transfer to St. Joseph's Seminary in Edmonton. It was not until 1951 that the theological work of a major seminary was provided by Christ the King. At least part of the reason for the late entry of Roman Catholics into the development of a full-fledged seminary can be seen when one considers the relatively small percentage of Catholics in the lower mainland in 1931. According to the 1931 census, approximately 50 percent of BC's population identified themselves as either Anglican or United Church, whereas only 14 percent of the population was Roman Catholic. According to the 1981 census, Roman Catholics constitute the largest religious denomination in Canada as a whole and in every province except BC. It is this fact that has affected its participation in higher education in BC.[19]

When the Seminary of Christ the King moved from Ladner to New Westminster and became a minor seminary, Dr. Leonard Klinck, the president of UBC from 1919 to 1944, was invited to speak at the opening ceremony. He expressed regret that so significant an educational institution was not being placed on the campus of the university. But since it was the Archbishop's intention to establish a Catholic university in BC at some time in the future, no effort had been made to place the diocesan seminary on the campus of a secular university or to seek affiliation with UBC. Indeed, shortly after Christ the King became a major seminary in 1951, the Benedictines, who staffed the Seminary, established Westminster Abbey in Mission, 45 miles up the Fraser river from Vancouver. They moved the Seminary of Christ the King to that site. The removal of the seminary to an isolated rural area made affiliation with UBC even less likely, and it created financial difficulties when, in 1952, the provincial government decided to make grants only to colleges affiliated with the single provincial university. It was not until the 1960s, when the government abandoned its "one university" policy and began granting charters to Simon Fraser University and the University of Victoria, that the Seminary of Christ the King finally received a charter empowering it to grant degrees in arts and theology.[20]

While the establishment of a diocesan seminary solved the practical problem of providing a training facility for Roman Catholic clergy in BC, its lack of affiliation with UBC created another set of problems when it came to providing for the higher education of Catholic laity. With its "one university" policy, the provincial government was not prepared to grant a charter to a separate Catholic university. Moreover, the university was not prepared to accept a federated Catholic liberal arts college on an arrangement similar to St. Michael's College in Toronto or St. Thomas More College in Saskatoon. There was a strong body of opinion within both the university and its alumni association that believed there was no room for sectarian higher education in BC. Initially, the only alternative that the university senate was prepared to entertain was a Catholic theological college on the model of the two Protestant colleges and they were prepared to grant such a college a similar lease on five acres of property in Theological Square, as well as affiliation with UBC. But since the Roman Catholics already had a diocesan seminary, they did not need what the senate was prepared to grant. What they needed was a liberal arts college for Catholic laity, but in view of the government's policy and the university's attitude, this first attempt to establish a Catholic college in 1937 was abandoned.[21]

The needs of the Catholic community, however, could not be permanently put on hold. Thus, when Dr. Norman MacKenzie became the president of UBC in 1944, another attempt was made to resolve the question. During his years as a professor of international law at the University of Toronto, MacKenzie had become familiar with St. Michael's University in Toronto and with Henry Carr, CSB. Carr had worked out the details of the federation between St. Michael's and the University of Toronto, and as Superior General of the Basilians had negotiated the federation of St. Thomas More College with the University of Saskatchewan. Archbishop Duke of Vancouver asked Father Carr to assist him in the negotiations with UBC. Almost immediately, however, both Dr. MacKenzie and Father Carr discovered that nothing had changed either the university's or the government's attitude on this question. Consequently, after a number of years of fruitless negotiation, Dr. MacKenzie finally suggested in 1951 that if a Catholic chaplain were appointed to staff the Newman Club, the campus organization for Roman Catholic students, he would look into the possibility of such a chaplain teaching a credit course in the university.[22]

The Basilians responded by appointing Carr as chaplain. MacKenzie made arrangements with Professor Logan, the head of the Classics Department, for Carr to teach two half courses, one in Latin and one in Greek. When Carr showed up to teach in a clerical collar, MacKenzie informed him that if he taught in lay attire he could confirm his appointment immediately, but if he insisted on wearing clerical dress he would have to put his appointment on hold until the Senate had discussed the matter further. Carr agreed to teach in lay dress but this annoyed Catholic students. When the incident was eventually picked up by the *Daily Province*, the pettiness of the Senate's action became public knowledge. As a result of this public airing of the issue, Carr's appointment was finally confirmed without restrictions.

Following this incident, an arrangement was devised whereby St. Mark's College would be granted a charter as a theological school affiliated with UBC and it would receive a five-acre site in the Theological Square of the university campus. It would not, however, function as a theological seminary. Instead, several members of the Basilian order would be appointed to teaching positions in the departments of history, economics, philosophy, and religious studies. This modus vivendi with the university was accepted as the best compromise possible after 14 years of negotiations, but it was an extremely precarious compromise. There were no guarantees on the university's part that the Basilian appointments were permanent. St. Mark's College continued to give Roman Catholics a presence on the campus and a centre for the Newman Club, but the university eventually withdrew from its earlier commitment to hire Basilians to teach in the Faculty of Arts.

The Founding and Growth of the Religious Studies Department at UBC

Beginning in the 1960s, a number of major changes took place in the institutional pattern for the study of religion just described. They were triggered by the Macdonald Report on Higher Education in British Columbia.[23] This report recommended the establishment of one university, two four-year colleges, and a system of regional two-year colleges throughout the province. The report was published in January of 1963, and in March of the same year the legislature passed a new Universities Act creating Simon Fraser University, University of Victoria, and Notre Dame University, as well as laying the foundations for a provincial network of community colleges that now number fifteen. These institutions have had no major impact on the study of religion in BC, since none of them developed a religious studies department and none has affiliated theological colleges, but they provided a clear indication that the province had abandoned its "one university" policy in higher education. This, in turn, led to the abandonment of the "anti-sectarian" policy, a development that had a significant influence on the study of religion in the province.

The effort to build religious studies into the institutional framework of UBC started well before its eventual success in the 1960s. In the United States during the post-World War II period, many became dissatisfied with the granting of transfer credit for religion courses taught in denominational colleges because, while it was understood that instruction in such courses had to be nonsectarian, it nevertheless "set the study of religion apart from the regular curriculum and stamped the courses with a sectarian image."[24] Many at UBC agreed with this view and wanted the university to establish its own Department of Religious Studies to provide not only electives for undergraduates, but also the possibility of doing majors and honours work at the undergraduate level and ultimately both an MA and a PhD program at the graduate level. Thus, a year after the Senate accepted the "Iowa Plan" Committee's report, and before it was fully implemented, a meeting of the Faculty of Arts and Sciences on 18 January 1956 approved a motion from R.M. Clark (Economics) and F.H. Soward (History) requesting the dean to appoint a committee "to consider the advisability of recommending to the Senate and Board of Governors the establishment of a Department of Religious Studies."[25]

Part of the reason for this motion was that an ad hoc legal committee of the Senate had ruled in August 1955 against one of the courses proposed by the theological colleges. The course, entitled "Foundations of Christianity," had as its objective the study of basic Christian doctrines such as the existence of God, the Trinity, and the Sacraments. When this course was referred to the legal firm of Sutton, Braidwood, Morris and Hall for an opinion, W.A. Sutton reported that there was "a dearth of Canadian and English cases as to the meaning of 'sectarian'," and as a result he had been forced to rely on the New Oxford Dictionary for the definition of such terms as "creed," "dogma," and "sectarian" and to commentary on a variety of American cases. From these sources, he concluded that "a generalized approach to religion is not in error under our Statute [i.e., Section 99 of the University Act] but the teaching of any such subject should not be carried out in such a manner as to indoctrinate or inculcate into the mind of the student, any particular religious creed or dogma."[26] On the basis of this report the ad hoc committee concluded that the proposed course was "not in accordance with the terms of the University Act."[27]

In response to this decision, and at the initiative of the Faculty of Arts and Science, Dr. MacKenzie began, in October 1956, to contact a number of acquaintances concerning the establishment of a Department of Religious Studies at UBC and to ask for the names of those who could establish such a department.[28] These enquiries, however, did not produce an acceptable candidate. It was not until 1958, therefore, when the president established a Committee for an Appointment in Religious Studies, that the search developed some momentum.[29] William Nicholls, former Anglican chaplain at the University of Edinburgh, was appointed as a tenured full professor, effective 1 May 1961.

Since there was no Department of Religious Studies as yet, Nicholls's first task was to make a proposal to the Senate on the establishment of a department. In November 1961, he presented to the Senate "A Memorandum on Policy, and a Sketch of Possible Future Development" for a Department of Religious Studies.[30] The report requested departmental status for religious studies, the removal of restrictions confining students to two courses in religious studies, and the appointment of an assistant professor in the biblical field for 1962-63. All of Nicholls's requests were granted except departmental status. Before granting this request, the Senate wanted further information on how religious studies was being handled in all other Canadian universities. This request was probably a stalling tactic on the part of those who were not yet convinced that UBC needed a Department of Religious Studies. But having been given two out of three items on his list, Nicholls complied with this request and by 19 January 1962 a copy of his "Summary of Provisions for Religious Studies in Canadian Universities" was on the president's desk and ready for distribution to the registrar and the Senate.[31] Meanwhile Nicholls launched a search for an assistant professor in the biblical field, and Charles P. Anderson was appointed on 1 July 1962.

Six months later, Nicholls again requested from the Senate departmental status, further appointments, and approval for a major in religious studies. Since the Faculty of Arts and Science had already approved it, the Senate granted this request, but still hesitated on departmental status and further appointments. Progress was made on another crucial matter, the amendment to Section 99 of the University Act. As originally passed, Section 99 stated that "The University shall be strictly non-sectarian in principle, and no religious creed or dogma shall be taught." In an amendment passed by the Legislative Assembly in 1963, the word "inculcated" was substituted for the word "taught," in order to remove any doubts about the legality of religious studies.[32] With the University Act amended, it was possible for the Senate to approve the establishment of a Department of Religious Studies at UBC. This took place on 20 May 1964; the Board of Governors also approved Nicholls's appointment without term as head of the department. Hanna Kassis and Arthur Link were appointed to professorial positions on 1 July 1964.

Once the department had a complement of four full-time members and was able to offer a major and honours program, it became evident that the university had two incompatible programs in religious studies: the old "Iowa Plan" arrangement with the theological colleges and the new Department of Religious Studies. To resolve this situation, Dr. R.M. Healy, the acting dean of Arts, set up the Eliot Committee to work out a way to terminate the old Religious Knowledge Option courses.[33] By 25 July 1965, the committee recommended that the RKO courses should be phased out by the end of the academic year 1967-68, that the theological colleges would have the right to propose courses for credit in Arts, that these courses would be handled by the curriculum committee of the Faculty of Arts, and that it would refer them to the appropriate department for approval in the same manner as all proposals for new courses. If these courses received the approval of the Faculty of Arts and the Senate, then the sponsoring department would have the same academic responsibility for them as for the regular departmental offerings.[34] With the acceptance of this report, the Department of Religious Studies was finally ready to move forward in what everyone assumed would be a normal course of development.

No one, however, appears to have anticipated what would happen in a department like religious studies when the "baby-boom" generation arrived at the university in the late 1960s. From an enrollment of 152 in 1964 when the department was established, student numbers ballooned to 882 five years later. Even with the appointment of J.I. Richardson in Hinduism on 1 July 1967 and Shotaro Iida in Buddhism a year later, the department had difficulties coping with this influx of students. As a result, it appeared as if Nicholls's earlier estimate of an eight-member department in perhaps a decade would be reached in half that time. But just as no one had predicted the rapid increase, no one seemed to realize how unstable and temporary this growth would be. Students began to disappear from the department almost as quickly as they had arrived. By 1975 enrollment in Religious Studies was down to 388, and by 1980 it had dropped to 240. In the meantime, new appointments had been made in Christianity, Hebrew Bible, Judaism, and Buddhism. By 1975 the department had nine-and-a-half full-time faculty members, while undergraduate enrollment continued to fall. The introduction of the MA in religious studies and the PhD in Buddhism helped to justify a larger teaching staff, but ultimately the shift in student interest from Eastern to Western religions in the late 1970s left the Eastern side of the program vulnerable, especially when graduate work in these areas did not expand at the rate that had been anticipated.[35]

Throughout the late 1970s and the early 1980s, tensions and conflict developed between Nicholls and the other members of the Department of Religious Studies. In 1983, Dean of Arts Robert M. Will initiated a full-scale departmental review. He appointed a committee to conduct the review of the department's graduate and undergraduate programs, the quality of teaching, the scholarly activity of the department, its administration, enrollments, facilities, and any other matters the committee deemed relevant.[36] The committee conducted extensive personal interviews with all members of the department and sought advice from three external consultants: Robert Cully of McGill, Steven Wilson of Carleton, and Masa Nagatomi of Harvard. The committee also sent out questionnaires to six representative Departments of Religious Studies in North America and received detailed replies from three of them. On the basis of these materials, the committee drafted its report and submitted it to the Dean of Arts on 31 December 1983.

The report focused on three general areas: governance, scholarship, and teaching. What was said about the governance of the department is not known because, when Nicholls resigned as head of the department after reading the report, it was agreed that this section would remain confidential. The sections on scholarship and teaching, however, were sent to members of the department on 9 January 1984. With regard to scholarship, the publication record of the department as a whole was judged to be less than adequate and well below the standards set by other university departments. The committee's view of the department's teaching and curriculum was also critical. These findings, therefore, led to the inevitable conclusion that the department should be disbanded as soon as possible.

All departmental review committees at UBC are set up to advise the dean, and he is free to accept or reject the advice given. In this case, the dean accepted Nicholls's resignation, but he did not accept the committee's recommendation that the department be disbanded. Instead, he appointed Daniel Overmyer of the Asian Studies Department as the temporary head of religious studies, and he solicited the department's cooperation in rectifying specific curricular and administrative problems referred to in the report. Overmyer was a graduate of the History of Religions program at the University of Chicago and he was seen as a friend of the department. Consequently, he received the full and immediate cooperation of all members of the department in dealing with these problems.

The financial restraints faced by the university, however, led to drastic actions that threatened the future of the department. In 1985, Dean Will was asked to respond to a series of general and specific questions about a number of units and programs within the Faculty of Arts. Specific reference was made to the report on the Department of Religious Studies. The request stated: "In light of the committee's findings, please show cause why this department should not be considered for discontinuance."[37] There were a number of departments mentioned in this letter, but the only other one being considered for discontinuance was the School of Family and Nutritional Sciences, which was in a better position than religious studies because it had not received a negative review.

Dean Will consulted with the department. Dan Overmyer replied that the review committee's report was out of date and did not accurately reflect the current situation in the department. Overmyer included with his own letter a document prepared by Charles Anderson which argued that the Department of Religious Studies at UBC was the only one of its kind in the province, and if it were discontinued, BC would be the only province in Canada without a centre for the objective and comparative study of religious phenomena. Overmyer concluded that "there are many good reasons for keeping and strengthening the department, and none for discontinuing it."[38]

Besides this formal exchange of letters, individual members of the department wrote letters to various religious groups, inter-faith organizations, and faculty members requesting support in heading off this threat to the department's existence. While the department appreciated the efforts of those who took the time to express their support, they had to admit that these responses did not add up to a great ground swell of confidence from the community. Indeed, this exercise produced some painful truths that had to faced. First, 90 percent of the university's faculty outside of Arts did not know that such a department existed or were unable to distinguish it from the work of the theological colleges. While there was a higher degree of recognition within the Faculty of Arts, there was still considerable confusion over the department's function, and there were very few who were prepared to stand up and be counted as supporters, especially if this might mean cuts in their own departmental budgets. Another part of the problem was that most academics in the humanities and social sciences had accepted the widely held view that industrialized societies were becoming increasingly secular and those who remain religious in this environment tended to belong to an underclass of immigrant communities and marginalized individuals. From this perspective, therefore, religion was an increasingly diminishing and irrelevant factor in modern and modernizing societies and religious studies had become a peripheral element in a university curriculum with a financial base that was shrinking at an alarming rate.[39]

In the community outside the university, the problem was somewhat different. Here there was a greater readiness to acknowledge the importance of religion, especially one's own religion. But the idea of treating all the major world religions as equally valid cultural expressions struck many as incomprehensible. The problem many perceived with this approach to the study of religion was that it not only undermined the fundamental assumptions on which centuries of Christian missions had rested, but also it relativised the central claims of the Christian doctrine of revelation. Interestingly, one of the few groups that fully supported the Department of Religious Studies was the Jewish community because they realized that the department provided the only context at the university level in BC where Judaism could be taught as something more than a precursor of Christianity and where its students would not be exposed to Christian proselytizing.

All of these efforts to save the department, however, appeared to have failed when, on 15 May 1985, its members were called into the dean's office and informed that the Department of Religious Studies was to be eliminated that June. All members of the staff were to be dismissed from their teaching positions. Three days later, however, the dean called to inform everyone that a different financial solution had been found and that the department would not be eliminated.

After the department's brush with extinction in 1985, a number of significant changes took place. First, three members of the department were promoted to full professor and one to associate professor by university committees that looked at their scholarship and publication records from a balanced perspective. Second, enrollment patterns appeared to turn around and the department recovered from the low point of its enrollment in 1979.[40] Third, the department's ability to attract first-class graduate students has became apparent when Elizabeth Anne MacDonald, one of the department's MA candidates, won the 1989 Governor-General's Gold Medal.

The department's publication record also dramatically improved after 1985. The English and Spanish editions of Hanna Kassis' *A Concordance of the Qur'an* received widespread international acclaim.[41] Furthermore, two colleagues of Arthur Link, who died before his massive work on the lives of 350 eminent Buddhist monks in China between 100 BC and 400 AD could be published, have undertaken the task of preparing this manuscript for publication. It will appear over the next few years in six volumes.[42] N. Keith Clifford published a major study of the resistance to church union in Canada with the University of British Columbia Press.[43] These works, together with articles and papers produced by all members of the department, significantly increased the department's visibility both nationally and internationally. It demonstrated that its scholarship met the highest standards established in the various areas of specialization within the field.

It is evident from the early records that those who advocated the establishment of a Department of Religious Studies at UBC were convinced that religion was an important aspect of culture. It is also evident that prior to the establishment of the department, considerable time was spent on the question of how religion ought to be studied and taught in a provincial university that was supported by public funds. The key term used in the early documents was that religion should not be "inculcated" and no attempt should be made to "indoctrinate" students into the tenets of any particular religion. To ensure that no indoctrination took place, the department made it clear that it would teach not one but five of the major world religions. Moreover, each of these religions would be presented as equally valid cultural products and no attempt would be made to argue that one was superior to the others. It was these decisions, most of which were made by the university prior to the establishment of the department, that clearly distinguished it from the theological colleges and placed it firmly within the orbit of the Faculty of Arts and in relation to all those departments that were involved in the study of culture.

There is no evidence that those who established the department were consciously attempting to devise an approach to the study of religion that would be appropriate to the new type of pluralistic society emerging on the West Coast of Canada. But this is in fact what they did. The university did not see itself supporting any religion. Its intention was to establish a non-sectarian approach to the study of the world's religions. Thirty years later, however, it has become apparent that what were viewed formerly as exotic religions from faraway places, have now suddenly become part of the social fabric of BC. The religions of the world are now on our doorstep; their houses of worship are part of our landscape providing, forceful reminders that these new religious communities are here to stay and their adherents expect to be treated not as strangers at our gates, but as major contributors to Canadian society.[44]

Christianity is still the dominant religion in BC and it is appropriate that the theological colleges of the major Christian groups in the province are affiliated with the university. But their task is quite different from that of the Department of Religious Studies. Their role is the advocacy of a particular religious tradition and the formation of professional practitioners in that tradition. Like the departments of political science and economics, which pursue the critical study of all political and economic theories, the Department of Religious Studies pursues the critical study of all the major religious traditions and has no interest in the "advocacy," "indoctrination," or "inculcation" of any type of religious belief or practice. Its interests are purely academic and it has nothing whatever to do with the professional training of ministers.

The Growth of Theological Studies for Conservative Evangelicals

With the demise of the Vancouver Bible Training College in the 1950s, the educational activities of the Protestant evangelical community in the lower mainland had reverted to denominational control. Most of these denominations were small, however, and their constituencies could not provide sufficient funds to develop first-class institutions; training for missionaries and church workers, therefore, left much to be desired. It was E. Marshall Sheppard, a local shoe merchant and recognized leader among the Plymouth Brethren assemblies in Vancouver and Victoria, who laid the foundations of a major institution that could serve the needs of a broad evangelical conservative community in BC. Sheppard had been a strong supporter of the Vancouver Bible Training College and a personal friend of its principal, Walter Ellis. Although elements within the Plymouth Brethren were considered by many to be among the most anti-intellectual segments of the evangelical community, Sheppard actively campaigned in both his own denomination and in wider evangelical circles for the establishment of a graduate school of theology in the Vancouver area.

Sheppard's proposal was discussed at the Inter-Varsity Christian Fellowship's Urbana '64 convention with Ward Gasque and a number of other Brethren delegates.[45] As a result of these discussions, a Vancouver committee, with Sheppard as chair, was established to explore this proposal further. Since there was no distinction made between clergy and laity in the Brethren assemblies, the Vancouver committee were not interested in establishing a theological college for the professional training of ministers. On the other hand, the committee wanted something more than a bible college, because what they had in mind was a post-baccalaureate or graduate institute. Shortly after clarifying these goals, Ward Gasque, who had worked closely with the Vancouver committee from the beginning, met James H. Houston in Britain; in 1966 he wrote to the committee suggesting that Houston would be an ideal candidate for principal of their school. Gasque's opinion was later endorsed by F.F. Bruce, a noted Brethren scholar from the University of Manchester.

In 1967 Houston came to Vancouver for discussions with the local committee. For some time prior to these discussions, Houston had been thinking about the establishment of such a school in North America. As a result he had a very clear conception of the type of school that was needed. In his view, it would first have to be located on a university campus and be affiliated with that university; second, it must be a post-baccalaureate school; and third, it would have to be transdenominational in character. While the first and third suggestions were somewhat beyond the point the committee had reached in its thinking, they were sufficiently impressed by Houston's ideas to invite him to become the first principal. In 1968 this institution was incorporated as Regent College and given degree-granting powers. In 1969 and 1970 successful summer schools were held prior to the opening of the college for full-time study in the fall of 1970. Houston was appointed as principal, Drs. W.J. Martin and S.M. Block as vice-principals, and Carl Armerding and Ward Gasque as assistant professors.

For the first few years, the college held its classes in the basement of Union College. The first program offered was a one-year Diploma in Christian Studies. In the second year this program was expanded to a two-year Master of Christian Studies degree program. Initially, the majority of the student body came from

Brethren background but very quickly a significant number of students from other denominations such as the Christian Missionary Alliance, the Evangelical Free Church, and the Mennonite and Pentecostal Churches augmented the college's enrollment. Regent College was not seen as a threat to either the Anglican or United Church theological colleges in the early stages of its development because it was serving a different constituency, was not involved in professional education for the ministry, and was offering different degrees. Thus, affiliation with the VST met with little difficulty in 1972. But the affiliation of Regent College with UBC in the same year was another matter.

In the Faculty of Arts and the Senate there were a number of individuals who took exception to the fact that Regent College required its faculty to subscribe to the doctrinal statement of the World Evangelical Fellowship which the college had adopted as its own. Subscription to a doctrinal statement and an emphasis on personal religious conviction and commitment, it was argued, were incompatible with "free academic enquiry." Although this viewpoint was powerfully represented in the Faculty of Arts committee that was formed to consider the affiliation of Regent College, the majority of the committee came to the conclusion that if this argument were generally applied to Roman Catholics, Communists, Freudians, or to any sufficiently dogmatic adherent of a set of beliefs, it would become an excuse for limiting free enquiry rather than a defence of it.[46] Not everyone in the Faculty of Arts or the Senate agreed with the committee's conclusion that "the principle of open enquiry itself, therefore, prevented the committee from concluding that the aims and beliefs of the college should be seized on as a barrier to affiliation."[47] As a result the issue generated much heated debate, but in the end the majority opinion of the committee prevailed and Regent College was granted affiliation with UBC in 1972.

By 1975 Regent College had outgrown its rented accommodation in the basement of VST and it moved into two converted fraternity houses on the edge of the campus. Much of its rapid growth is attributable to the fact that many from a broad spectrum of evangelical denominations turned to Regent for training prior to entering the ministry of their respective churches. The use of the college for this purpose created difficulties, because James Houston's original vision was that its emphasis would be on lay training rather than professional training for ministers. The need for a major evangelical theological college in western Canada, however, was so great that it placed pressure on Regent College to develop in this direction and to provide professional degrees such as the MDiv. After a decade as principal, James Houston maintained his original conviction that Regent College should not contribute to the increasing professionalization of the ministry in Canadian church life and society. From the beginning of his association with the school he had maintained that Regent College should function as a graduate lay training centre. But the constituency of Regent College had changed in the decade since its founding, and the educational requirements of the Plymouth Brethren were not the only needs that had to be met. Therefore, rather than create serious divisions within the college, Houston stepped aside in 1978 and Carl Armerding was appointed principal, with Houston assuming the newly created position of chancellor.

In 1979 the MDiv program was introduced and affiliation with VST was terminated, for it placed Regent College and the VST in direct competition as centres of professional education for ministry. This shift of emphasis at Regent College came at a time when an increasing number of evangelicals were applying for ordination in the United Church of Canada. The United Church was prepared to accept them as candidates provided they took their training in theological colleges recognized by the United Church of Canada. But shortly after Regent College launched its MDiv program, Dr. Howie Mills, the secretary of the Division of Ministry, Personnel and Education for the United Church, made it very clear that anyone trained at Regent College would not be accepted for ordination by the United Church. The reaction of the Anglican and Presbyterian Churches was less direct, but many within these denominations had similar views.

From the perspective of the Department of Religious Studies, the transformation of Regent College into a theological seminary presented no problems whatever. Indeed, this was an improvement over Houston's vision for Regent College because one of the features of his dream was a negative view of all departments of religious studies. This view was not based on personal animosity toward any member of the UBC department, but on the conception of departments of religious studies. In 1974, he spelled this out:

> My own conviction was that the development of departments of religious studies replacing the more denominational and professional activities of previous theological education on secular campuses might break up, as it became obvious that such departments lacked adequate coherence and unity. If, then, these were replaced by such more specialized institutes of Jewish, Buddhist or Islamic studies, we could always assume to be no more than an institute of Christian studies.[48]

At the methodological level there was in fact much more unity and coherence in the Department of Religious Studies than Houston perceived, for every member of the department was trained in the historical method and its ancillary disciplines and all were textually oriented in their approach to the five major world religions.[49] The type of unity and coherence envisioned by Houston, however, was not academic. It was based on an evangelical version of Christianity which has serious reservations about the validity of Catholic, Orthodox, and liberal Protestant Christian witness. It was this type of sectarianism, however, that the university had been determined to avoid when it established the Department of Religious Studies, and the prospect of separate Buddhist, Christian, Hindu, Islamic, and Jewish institutes on the campus would have struck the founders of the department as a sectarian nightmare rather than a vision with which the university could identify. Thus, when Regent College became an identifiable professional school, some breathed a sigh of relief, for this was an identity that the university could comprehend and accept.

In 1980 Regent College affiliated with Carey Hall, the college of the Baptist Union of Western Canada, which originally had been intended to serve as a seminary. The idea behind this affiliation was that Carey Hall would provide the pastoral courses necessary for their new professional program, while Regent College would continue to provide the academic courses in the biblical, theological, and historical fields. This arrangement made it possible for Regent College to become a fully accredited member of the ATS in 1985, just six years, rather than six decades, following its move into professional education for ministers. Finally, in September 1988, it moved out of its cramped quarters in fraternity houses and into an impressive new building that was paid for before it opened. It also welcomed a new principal, Dr. Walter Wright, who was recruited from the faculty of Fuller Theological Seminary. Thus, by 1989,

Regent College had become a firmly established theological college serving the needs of the evangelical community in BC and western Canada as well as attracting many from further afield because of the reputation of its faculty.

Another institution that began to take shape in the 1960s and that revealed the growing strength and influence of the evangelical Protestant community in British Columbia was Trinity Western University at Langley, BC. It began in 1962 as a two-year college of the Evangelical Free Church, a small denomination of Scandinavian background, and it expanded very rapidly. Its enrollment increased from 17 in the first year to 350 in 1970 and over 1,100 by 1986.[50] Part of the reason for its success was that it provided Evangelicals with access to a college, rather than a bible school, education in a "safe" environment designed to strengthen their faith and pietistic standards of conduct rather than undermine them in the secular and pluralistic environment of the provincial universities. A Christian environment was established by requiring the faculty to subscribe to an evangelical statement of faith and conduct and by insisting that the Christian presuppositions and implications of each subject be clearly articulated in order to achieve an integration of faith and learning.[51] These principles appealed to a much wider spectrum of the evangelical community than the Evangelical Free Church alone, and as a result students from the Baptist, Mennonite, Pentecostal, and Christian and Missionary Alliance denominations soon formed a majority of its student body.

By 1977, Trinity Western College was allowed to introduce a four-year program and in 1979 it was authorized to grant degrees. Since the NDP government, which was in power from 1972 to 1975, opposed the college's expansion to a four-year program with degree-granting status, and since the Universities Council of British Columbia opposed the basic principles of the college (the faculty had to subscribe to the college's statement of faith; bible study was compulsory for all students; and courses in biology stressed creationist rather than evolutionary theory), Trinity Western supporters began in 1975 to work for the defeat of the NDP government and to lobby Social Credit MLAs for support of a private member's bill that would enable the college to achieve its objectives.

Following the defeat of the NDP government in 1975, extensive lobbying was carried on among the Social Credit MLAs, and in 1977 Trinity Western was granted half of its ultimate objective (i.e., four-year status). It took a further two years, however, to obtain degree-granting powers. By emphasizing that the private nature of the college would not make it a drain on the public purse, it was possible to get the full attention of a government that was trying to cut the costs of education in BC and to persuade them to give the college degree-granting status.[52] This action produced widespread public controversy.

The basic issue was that since Trinity Western was a private, church-related college, authorizing it to grant degrees violated the province's earlier "anti-sectarian" policy in higher education. The bible colleges had been parallel but not equal institutions and did not have degree-granting powers. The anti-sectarianist view was that once these powers were given to a private, church-related institution, there could be no obstacles, other than financial, to other religious groups establishing educational institutions that would be both parallel and equal to the public universities and colleges. This apprehension had proved to be well founded as the modified policy had the full support of the Social Credit government, and it had been in effect ever since 1963 when Notre Dame College in Nelson had been given degree-granting powers and a year later Christ the King Seminary at Mission had been authorized to grant a BA degree. Moreover, the NDP opposition was split on the issue because Dave Barrett, MLA, having received his university training at an American Catholic college, had no objection to the principle of sectarian or church-related higher education. Consequently, the public controversy over the question did little more than allow those who opposed sectarian higher education to voice their opinions. By 1984, when Trinity Western was given membership in the Association of Universities and Colleges of Canada, the issue was settled; the following year Trinity Western College changed its name to Trinity Western University in order to clarify its new standing among the educational institutions of BC.

A comparison of religious studies at Trinity Western and UBC reveals some interesting differences. Religious studies at UBC is a program that students may choose if they wish to know something about religion. But at Trinity Western, twelve units of courses in religious studies are required for graduation in all degree programs. Moreover, rather than being a department within the Arts Faculty as it is at UBC, religious studies at Trinity Western is one of the eight divisions and therefore it is equal in status to the other divisions of the social sciences, humanities, and natural sciences. Furthermore, since the Division of Religious Studies must service the entire student body of 1,100 rather than the two percent of the UBC student body that the Department of Religious Studies serves, the faculty in the Division of Religious Studies at Trinity Western is larger than that of UBC's Department of Religious Studies. At Trinity there are eight full-time faculty and two part-time lecturers, while UBC currently has only four full-time members and five part-time instructors. Finally, differences in the assumptions behind the two approaches to religious studies stand in stark contrast to one another. At UBC the emphasis is placed on the objective study of religion. At Trinity Western, the Calendar makes it clear that biblical study "should never be approached purely objectively; God is to be encountered, not just discussed and the Scriptures obeyed, not just read."[53]

A recent development in connection with Trinity Western University indicated that Regent College was not able to meet all the needs of the conservative evangelical community in BC for professional theological education. In 1987, three small theological schools, the well-established Northwest Baptist Seminary, the newly created Canadian Evangelical Free Church Seminary, and the Canadian Baptist Seminary, affiliated with Trinity Western University and located on the Langley campus. This development in theological education is so recent that it is difficult to determine its significance for the evangelical community in general or for Regent College in particular. It is necessary to observe that some members of this community are more comfortable in a rural rather than an urban environment and some are still culturally alienated from the secular pluralistic world of the public university. As a result, they are unwilling to enter into an affiliation with UBC as have the other theological colleges. At the moment these differences do not appear to represent major divisions among evangelicals; they simply reflect differences in the orientation and ethos of the denominations supporting these institutions. Whether these differences will lead to problems in the future, of course, remains to be seen.

Regent and Trinity Western did not satisfy the needs of all conservative evangelicals in BC. A number of bible colleges and institutes, founded earlier in the century, expanded their programs when the province began to approve degree-granting charters to institutions other than UBC. Mennonites had founded colleges in the

Fraser Valley since the 1930s. In 1970, the Mennonite Brethren Bible Institute and the Bethel Bible Institute merged to form the Columbia Bible Institute in Clearbrook. The name changed to Columbia Bible College in 1987 when the province granted the college the right to grant theological degrees. Northwest Baptist Theological College was opened by the Regular Baptists in Coquitlam in 1945 as Northwest Bible College. It moved to Vancouver in 1958 and to Langley as part of the Associated Canadian Theological Colleges at Trinity Western University in 1990. Western Pentecostal Bible College began as the British Columbia Bible Institute in Victoria in 1941, established by the Pentecostal Assemblies. It moved to North Vancouver in 1951 and to Clayburn in the Fraser Valley in 1974. The Pacific Bible College was an independent school founded in Vancouver in 1972. All of these institutions are accredited by the Association of Canadian Bible Colleges or the American Association of Bible Colleges.

New Directions in Mainline Protestant Theological Studies

The Vancouver School of Theology, which organically united the Anglican Theological College and Union College into a new entity, was also a product of the 1960s. From the time of their founding in BC, the theological colleges that evolved into VST had seen themselves as professional schools. Both Columbian College and Westminster Hall participated in the first major survey of theological colleges sponsored by the recently formed ATS in 1924,[54] and their successors have participated in all the ATS-sponsored studies in every decade since 1924.[55] Moreover, from 1927 onwards, both Union College and the Anglican Theological College had cooperated on curriculum, library resources, and teaching appointments. In spite of all this, however, it was apparent in 1962 from the ATS Visitors' Report, submitted by John Dillenberger and Robert T. Handy, that neither college could expect to receive full accreditation as long as they remained separate institutions.[56] The difficulty with associate membership in the ATS was that it implied second-class status and indicated that their degrees and training did not measure up to those offered by the fully accredited schools elsewhere in Canada and the United States.

How long it would have taken these schools to amalgamate if left on their own is not clear, but they received a gentle push in this direction as a result of studies launched by both the Canadian churches and the ATS in the 1960s. These studies came to the conclusion that there were too many small colleges in Canada training too few candidates for the ministry.[57] Out of these studies, a plan gradually emerged that recommended the closing of some Canadian schools and the clustering of others in major university centres. Since everyone agreed that Vancouver ought to be one of the centres, the idea of amalgamating the Anglican and United Colleges received strong support from denominational leaders and the college boards alike. The decision to move forward with this plan cleared the way for the emergence of the VST in 1971, with W.S. Taylor as its first principal, and laid the basis for its full accreditation in 1975. It had taken the mainline denominations eight decades to create a first-class, fully accredited professional school in BC. It is understandable, therefore, that some expressed shock and consternation when, four years later, Regent College announced that it was also about to move into the professional education of ministers.

At least part of the reason for the consternation at the VST was that all of the colleges that went into its formation were based on Canadian models. In contrast, Regent College moved from being a graduate lay training institute to being a theological college, adopting Fuller Theological Seminary in Pasadena, California as its model, and it appeared as if its intention was to become, like Fuller in the United States, the premier intellectual centre of neo-evangelicalism in Canada.[58] The anti-modernist stance of the bible colleges had never posed a threat to the theological colleges of the mainline denominations because the fundamentalists appeared to them to be nothing more than a backward-looking cultural minority who were extremely defensive and alienated from the dominant culture and the major Canadian universities. By 1978, however, the charismatic revival and the rise of neo-evangelicalism were already creating major problems within the mainline denominations that had been seriously weakened by dramatic and continuous losses in membership from the late 1960s onwards.[59] Rightly or wrongly, the Anglican and United theological colleges on campus were accustomed to seeing themselves as institutions that represented the cultural mainstream of Canadian life. Up until the mid-1960s, their non-sectarian Protestant assumptions had enabled them to reach a comfortable accommodation with UBC, especially in its public rituals such as the baccalaureate service and graduation ceremonies.

Moreover, in the establishment of the Department of Religious Studies, the university almost automatically appointed the principals of the two Protestant theological colleges to the committee, but did not invite the principal of St. Mark's to participate. By the late 1970s, however, the atmosphere on the university campus had changed. The university appeared to be much more in the "no-religion" camp representing the fastest-growing segment of BC society according to the census figures. Regent College represented a consortium of the new evangelicals, and VST the rapidly dwindling forces of the formerly dominant mainline churches.[60]

The Vancouver School of Theology did gain substantial ground under the leadership of James P. Martin, principal from 1972-83. He was responsible for hiring a new faculty and redesigning the curriculum, with particular attention being paid to the integration of the academic and practical dimensions of the professional education of the clergy. The appointment of Dr. Arthur Van Seters as the third principal of VST in 1983 underlined the school's continuing commitment to professional education. Prior to his arrival in Vancouver, Dr. Van Seters had been the director of the Montreal Institute for Ministry, which provided the pastoral training program for the Faculty of Religious Studies at McGill. Further developments in distance education, Native Indian ministries, and continuing education for ministers in the 1980s have made VST the best mainline Protestant theological college in western Canada and one of the strongest in the country.

The Vancouver School of Theology further strengthened its position in 1984 by affiliating with St. Andrew's Hall, the Presbyterian college on campus, which originally had also been established to educate clergy.[61] Through its affiliation with St. Andrew's Hall and the resulting association with the Presbyterian Church in Canada, VST became the western theological college for the three largest Protestant denominations in Canada and its faculty was strengthened by the addition of the Dean of St. Andrew's Hall, Canadian church historian Brian J. Fraser, to its teaching staff.

Being the first multidenominational theological school in Canada did present problems, however. For example, who has responsibility for its continued financial support? When denominations lack control, especially in periods of economic restraint, they tend to feel less responsibility for major funding. Moreover, since the school has often been far in advance of the laity on a number of social justice and lifestyle issues, some major financial contributors to the former denominational colleges have been somewhat less than enthusiastic in their support of the new school. This reticence on the part of some contributors, however, has not threatened the development of its basic program, but rather meant that the timetable for some new developments has had to be altered. The idea of an multidenominational seminary is new in Canada, but insofar as major American seminaries like Union Theological Seminary in New York have set extremely high standards for ministerial education and have weathered many periods of financial restraint, there is no reason to believe that VST's future will be any less secure once those in its denominational constituencies realize how much it has to offer not only to the future of theological education in BC but also to the redefinition of the relationship between the mainline churches and the mainstream of Canadian culture. Such leadership is sorely needed by the mainline churches, and if it does not come from this source it is difficult to see where else it could come from at the present time.

At present it appears that both of these approaches to the study of religion, theological studies and religious studies, will continue through the 1990s and possibly into the next century. They serve different purposes and, for the most part, different constituencies. The unique history of the development of higher education in the province, particularly the creation of a private university based on conservative evangelical Christian principles, gave theological studies a prominence in BC that is unique in the country. In addition, because of past difficulties and current government cuts in the funding of higher education, the theological colleges and private institutions seem at present to be in a much stronger position than the Department of Religious Studies at UBC. Whether this situation will continue indefinitely remains to be seen. It depends on whether the provincial government and the university realize that commitments to faith, no matter of what variety, must be comprehended by a disengaged examination of their dynamics and impacts.

Notes

1 H.M. Tory, "McGill University in British Columbia," *McGill University Magazine*, 5, 2 (May 1906):185-204.

2 See F.W. Peake, "Theological Education in British Columbia," *Canadian Journal of Theology*, 5, 4 (1959): 251-62, and Mary D. Burton, "The Anglican Theological College of British Columbia 1909-1927: Unity and Diversity" (M.A. thesis, University of Alberta, 1974).

3 Accounts of the histories of Union College are found in Peake, "Theological Education," and C.M. Stewart, *The Story of Union College* (Vancouver: Vancouver School of Theology, 1971).

4 The Canadian dimensions of these studies are summarized in Charles Fielding, "Twenty-Three Theological Schools: Aspects of Canadian Theological Education," *Canadian Journal of Theology*, 12, 4 (1966): 229-37.

5 See R. Cole Harris, "Locating the University of British Columbia," *BC Studies*, 32 (Winter 1976-1977): 106-25.

6 See H.T. Logan, *Tuum Est: A History of the University of British Columbia* (Vancouver: University of British Columbia, 1958), and William C. Gibson, *Wesbrook and His University* (Vancouver: The Library of the University of British Columbia, 1973).

7 See the United Church's *Report of the Special Committee on Theological Education 1941*, Board of Christian Education, Box 11, file 115, UCA, Toronto.

8 For the relevant documents concerning Dr. Brown and Union College, see the Board of Christian Education, Box 9, files 103-106, UCA. The letter from G. Harrison Villet to Frank Langford, 9 March 1938, in file 105 is particularly revealing of the seriousness of the situation.

9 William Stephens Taylor PhD, DD, (1905-) was born in India of missionary parents. After his ordination to the ministry of the United Church of Canada in 1930, he returned to India as an educational missionary and he eventually became acting principal of Indore College from 1944-46. He was appointed principal of Union College in 1948 and remained in this position until 1971 when he became the first principal of the Vancouver School of Theology. For biographical information on J.W. Grant, see *Who's Who in Religion 1975-1976* (Chicago: Marquis Who's Who, 1975), 218.

10 *The United Church of Canada Year Book 1949*, 93. For biographical information on MacKenzie, see P.B. Waite, *Lord of Point Grey: Larry MacKenzie of UBC* (Vancouver: University of British Columbia Press, 1987).

11 Ormonde Hall, "Religion and UBC," *The UBC Alumni Chronicle*, 6, 2 (June 1952): 13. For background on the development of religious studies in the United States, see John F. Wilson, "The Background and Present Context of the Study of Religion in Colleges and Universities," in *The Study of Religion in Colleges and Universities*, ed. Paul Ramsey and John F. Wilson (Princeton: Princeton University Press, 1970). This volume also contains an excellent bibliography on religion in colleges and universities.

12 See the "Report of the Iowa Plan Committee of the UBC Alumni Association," in the *Senate Records*, Box 32, file 8, UBC Archives. For further information on the "Iowa Plan" and comparisons with the "Toronto Plan" and the "Illinois Plan," see Franklin H. Littell, "Church, State, and University," in *Religion and*

the Public Order, ed. Donald A. Giannella (Chicago: University of Chicago Press, 1963), 78-98. See also M. Willard Lampe, *The Story of an Idea: The History of the School of Religion at the State University of Iowa* (Iowa City: State University of Iowa Extension Bulletin No. 704, 1955).

13 See *UBC Senate Minutes*, vol. 14 (9 February, 1955), 2125, UBC Archives.

14 *The United Church of Canada Year Book, 1959*, 103.

15 For further background on the Anglican Theological College, see *Via Media*, ed. E. Gale (Vancouver: Anglican Theological College, 1961).

16 For background materials on the Vancouver Bible Training College and its principal, Walter Ellis, see Robert K. Burkinshaw, "Strangers and Pilgrims in Lotus Land: Conservative Protestantism in British Columbia 1917-1981" (PhD thesis, University of British Columbia, 1988).

17 For the history of the Bible colleges in Canada, see H.W. Boon, "The Development of the Bible College or Institute in the United States and Canada since 1880 and Its Relation to the Field of Theological Education in America" (PhD thesis, New York University, 1950). See also Ben Harder, "The Bible Institute-College Movement in Canada," *Journal of the Canadian Church Historical Society*, 20, 3-4 (1978): 29-45.

18 For a thorough analysis of the nature of the Toronto Bible College during these years, see John G. Stackhouse, Jr., *Canadian Evangelicalism in the Twentieth Century* (Toronto: University of Toronto Press, 1993), 53-70.

19 See David R. Stone, "Religion in Canada: Findings from the 1981 Census," in *Yearbook of American and Canadian Churches 1984*, ed. Constant H. Jacquet, Jr. (Nashville: Abingdon Press, 1984), 261-64.

20 See Laurence K. Shook, *Catholic Post-Secondary Education in English-Speaking Canada: A History* (Toronto: University of Toronto Press, 1971). In 1989, the BTh in theology was abandoned in favour of the MDiv degree which is currently the professional degree offered by most theological schools in North America. See *BC Catholic*, 27 August 1989.

21 Bishop Martin M. Johnson took steps in 1950 to establish a Catholic college, Notre Dame, in Nelson, BC. In 1952 Gonzaga University in Spokane, Washington granted Notre Dame affiliation and recognized its first two years, but required students to transfer to Spokane for their third and fourth years. In 1953 Premier W.A.C. Bennett placed Notre Dame on the list of British Columbia institutions eligible for federal grants. But it was not until 1963 that the government changed its "one university" policy and gave Notre Dame a degree-granting charter. Five years later the institution was secularized and began receiving provincial grants. In 1977 Notre Dame was closed by the Social Credit government of Bill Bennett and he was violently jostled by protesters when he visited Nelson shortly after closure. In 1979 the university was reopened as the David Thompson University Centre, but in 1984 it was again closed. See Justine Hunter, "4th University Plans Rekindle Nelson's Anger at Campus Closure," *Vancouver Sun*, 21 March 1989.

22 For background on the formation of St. Mark's College, see Shook, *Catholic Post-Secondary Education*, 373ff., and James Hanrahan, "Father Carr in Vancouver: The Beginnings of Catholic Education at UBC," *Canadian Catholic Review* (December 1985): 14-20.

23 John B. Macdonald, *Higher Education in British Columbia and a Plan for the Future* (Vancouver: University of British Columbia, 1962). See also John B. Macdonald, "The West," *Changing Patterns of Higher Education in Canada*, ed. Robin Harris (Toronto: University of Toronto Press, 1966).

24 *Religious Studies in Public Universities*, ed. Milton D. McLean (Carbondale: Southern Illinois University Press, 1967), 4. For the best available bibliography on all aspects of religion and higher education, see William A. Clebsch and Rosemary Rader, "Religious Studies in American Colleges and Universities: A Preliminary Bibliography," *Religious Studies Review*, 1, 1 (September 1975): 50-60. Unfortunately, this bibliography has not been updated as far as I am aware, and it contains no materials on Canada. For an interpretive article based on this bibliography, see William A. Clebsch, "Religious Studies Now: Not Why Not? But Why Not Not?" *Religious Education*, 70, 3 (May-June 1975): 264-77.

25 See *Minutes of the Faculty of Arts and Sciences*, 18 January 1956, UBC Archives.

26 See the "Interim Report of the Legal Sub-committee of the Senate Committee on Religious Studies," 3 August 1955, in the *Senate Records*, Box 32, file 8, UBC Archives. W.A. Sutton's definition of "inculcate," a word taken from his survey of American cases, was important because it was later used in the 1963 amendment of the University Act, but his survey of the relevant American cases was very superficial. For a more adequate survey of the American legal decisions and the problems of definition involved, see George R. La Noue, "The Conditions of Public School Neutrality," *Religion and Public Education*, ed. Theodore R. Sizer (Boston: Houghton Mifflin, 1967), 22-36 and Harold Stahmer, "Defining Religion: Federal Aid and Academic Freedom," in Giannella, *Religion and Public Order*, 116-46. See also David W. Louisell and John H. Jackson, "Religion, Theology, and Public Education," *California Law Review*, 50, 5 (December, 1962): 751-99.

27 See G.F. Curtis to Dr. N.A.M. MacKenzie, 29 January 1960, in the *Senate Records*, Box 32, file 8, UBC Archives. The members of the legal subcommittee were Dean G.F. Curtis (chair), and Messrs. Ladner, Nemetz, Carrothers, and Bourne.

28 See Richard Gilman to N.A.M. MacKenzie, 5 October 1956, in the *President's Files*, microfilm roll #282, UBC Archives. Richard Gilman was the executive director of the National Council on Religion in Higher Education which had its headquarters in New York.

29 The search committee consisted of Dean Andrew (chair), Dean Chant, Principal W.S. Taylor of Union College, Principal Woodhouse of the Anglican Theological College, and Professors Clark (often acting chairman), Conway (secretary), Davies, Jennings, Bourne, and Shemilt. No minutes of this committee seem to have survived, but John S. Conway, "The Universities and Religious Studies," *Canadian Journal of Theology*, 5, 4 (1959): 269-72 provides a window into the thinking of at least one committee member during the period when the search for a head of the Department of Religious Studies was being conducted. Among the candidates interviewed for the position, James P. Martin, who would later become the principal of the Vancouver School of Theology, was the only Canadian considered but he did not receive the full support of the committee. Paul Holmer was invited to Vancouver for an interview, but Yale Uni-

versity made him an offer before UBC. had made up its mind. Clyde Manschreck of Duke University received the committee's unanimous recommendation for appointment on 5 April 1959, but turned down the offer in favour of an appointment at the Chicago Theological Seminary.

30 See *Senate Records*, Box 32, file 8, UBC Archives.

31 See MacKenzie to Nicholls, 7 February 1962, with an attached copy of the "Summary" in the *Senate Records*, Box 32, file 8. UBC Archives.

32 See William Nicholls, "The Role of a Department of Religion in a Canadian University," *The Making of Ministers: Essays on Clergy Training Today*, ed. Keith R. Bridston and Dwight W. Culver (Minneapolis: Augsburg Publishing House, 1964), 72-90. See also C.G.W. Nicholls, "The Church as a Problem to the University," *University and Church: Two Points of View* (Toronto: The Anglican Church of Canada, 1967), 3-18.

33 This committee consisted of C.W.J. Eliot of Classics (chair), the principals of the Anglican, Union and St. Mark's colleges, and professors Bongie of French, Nicholls of Religious Studies, and Winter of History.

34 See "Committee on Religious Knowledge Options," in the *Dean of Arts Files*, Faculty of Arts, UBC.

35 For an thorough analysis of the place of religion in the undergraduate curriculum of American colleges and universities, see Robert Michaelsen, "Religion in the Undergraduate Curriculum," ed. Bridston and Culver, *The Making of Ministers*, 43-71. From this analysis it is possible to see how unusual was the rapid development of Buddhist Studies at UBC.

36 The members of the committee were Professors Donald Patterson of Economics, Richard Sikora of Philosophy, Paul Stanwood of English, James Taylor of Law, and Richard Tees of Psychology (chair). See "Terms of Reference" in the *Report of the Review Committee on the Department of Religious Studies, 31 December 1983*.

37 R.H.T. Smith to R.M. Will, 5 February 1985, "Re: Academic and Budget Planning 1985-86 and Beyond," *Dean of Arts Files*, Faculty of Arts, UBC.

38 D. Overmyer to R.M. Will, 22 February 1985, *Dean of Arts Files*, Faculty of Arts, UBC.

39 For a critical analysis of this outlook, see Mary Douglas, "The Effects of Modernization on Religious Change," *Religion and America: Spirituality in a Secular Age*, ed. Mary Douglas and Stephen Tipton (Boston: Beacon Press, 1983), 25-43.

40 The 1992-93 enrollment figures of 788, of whom 40 are engaged in majors or honours programs in religious studies, indicates that the number of students has almost tripled since 1979.

41 Hanna Kassis, *A Concordance of the Qur'an* (Berkeley: University of California Press, 1983) and Hanna Kassis with Karl Kobbervig, *Concordancias del Coran* (Madrid: Instituto Hispano-arabe de Cultura, 1987).

42 See *Records of the Eminent Buddhist Monks in China from 100 B.C.-400 A.D.*, translated by Arthur Link and edited by Shotaro Iida and Leon Hurvitz (Berkeley: Asian Humanities Press, forthcoming).

43 N. Keith Clifford, *The Resistance to Church Union in Canada,, 1904-1939* (Vancouver: University of British Columbia Press, 1985).

44 See Philip Marchand, "Houses of Worship," *Western Living* (March 1985), 22ff. The buildings discussed in this article are the Chinese Buddhist Quen Yim Temple, the Ismaili Mosque, the Nanksar Gurdwara, Gursikh Temple, St. Pius X Catholic Church, and Westminster Abbey. In 1962 Wilfred Cantwell Smith, Birks Professor of Comparative Religion at McGill, predicted that Canadian society as a whole would become more religiously pluralistic, and he emphasized the important role that departments of religious studies would have in shaping a new consciousness appropriate to this new society. See W. Cantwell Smith, *The Faith of Other Men* (Toronto: CBC Publications, 1962). Charles P. Anderson and Joseph I. Richardson from the Religious Studies Department at UBC have contributed to this new consciousness by compiling the first book on the history of all the religious groups in British Columbia. See *Circle of Voices: A History of the Religious Communities of British Columbia,* ed. C.P. Anderson, T. Bose, and J.I. Richardson (Lantzville, BC: Oolichan Books, 1983).

45 For background materials on the establishment of Regent College, see Stackhouse, *Canadian Evangelicalism,* 154-64.

46 The members of the Faculty of Arts committee on the affiliation of Regent College were: D.G. Brown of Philosophy, N.K. Clifford of Religious Studies, A.E. Link of Religious Studies (chair), R.D. Nemser of English, and W.E. Willmot of Anthropology. The argument of the majority was formulated by Brown and the report was drafted by Nemser.

47 See the "Report of the Faculty of Arts Committee on Regent College's Request for Affiliation with UBC," November 1972, in the *Dean of Arts Files,* Faculty of Arts, UBC.

48 See James M. Houston, "The History and Assumptions of Regent College," papers contributed to the conference, Openness to the Future: A Prelude to Planning, held at Regent College, 1974, cited in John G. Stackhouse, Jr., "Proclaiming the Word: Canadian Evangelicalism Since the First World War" (PhD thesis, University of Chicago, 1987), 205-206.

49 For a helpful discussion of method in religious studies departments and new developments in this area, see Frank E. Reynolds, "Introduction," in *Anthropology and the Study of Religion,* ed. Robert L. Moore and Frank E. Reynolds (Chicago: Center for the Scientific Study of Religion, 1985), 1-8.

50 See Burkinshaw, "Strangers and Pilgrims," 318.

51 See Stackhouse, *Canadian Evangelicalism,* 162-64.

52 For an interesting analysis of the political aspects of this question, see Victor J. Guenther, "A Case Study in Policy Making: The Trinity College Act (1977)," an unpublished paper prepared for Education 554 in 1984 at UBC.

53 *Trinity Western University Calendar, 1989/90* (Langley: Trinity Western University Press, 1989), 62.

54 See Robert L. Kelly, *Theological Education in America* (New York: George Doran, 1924), 371-75.

55 See William Adams Brown and Mark A. May, *The Education of American Ministers,* 4 vols. (New York: The Institute of Social and Religious Research, 1934); H. Richard Niebuhr, *The Purpose of the Church and Its Ministry* (New York: Harper, 1956); H. Richard Niebuhr, Daniel Day Williams, and James Gustafson, *The Advancement of Theological Education* (New York: Harper,

1957); and *Ministry in America*, ed. David S. Schuller, Merton P. Slonmen, and Milo I. Brekke (San Francisco: Harper & Row, 1980).

56 See "Report of the Visitors to the Union Theological College of British Columbia, November 12-15, 1962," VST Archives.

57 See Charles R. Fielding, "Twenty-three Theological Schools: Aspects of Canadian Theological Education," *Canadian Journal of Theology*, 12 (1966), 229-37. See also Charles R. Fielding, *Education for Ministry* (Dayton: American Association of Theological Schools, 1966), and Harold W. Vaughan, *Theological Education in the United Church of Canada* (Toronto: United Church of Canada, 1967).

58 See George M. Marsden, *Reforming Fundamentalism: Fuller Seminary and the New Evangelicalism* (Grand Rapids: Eerdmans, 1988), for an insightful examination of the transition from fundamentalism to neo-evangelicalism and an excellent history of the role played by Fuller Seminary in this transition.

59 See Reginald W. Bibby, *Fragmented Gods: The Poverty and Potential of Religion in Canada* (Toronto: Irwin, 1987). In this study, I have focused on changes in British Columbia. For a broader analysis of such changes, see Martin E. Marty, "Religion in America Since Mid-century," in *Religion and America*, ed. Douglas and Tipton, 273-87.

60 See Richard Quebedeaux, *The Worldly Evangelicals* (New York: Harper & Row, 1978), and Wade Clark Roof and William McKinney, *American Mainline Religion: Its Changing Shape and Future* (New Brunswick: Rutgers University Press, 1987). See also Wade Clark Roof, "America's Voluntary Establishment: Mainline Religion in Transition," in *Religion and America*, ed. Douglas and Tipton, 47.

61 James Perry Martin (1923-) was born and educated in Vancouver. He received his BSc from UBC in 1946 and his theological and graduate training at Princeton Theological Seminary. He taught at Princeton from 1959 to 1962 and at Union Theological Seminary in Virginia from 1962 to 1972. He succeeded Dr. W.S. Taylor as the second principal of VST in 1972 and continued in this position until 1983. He retired in 1988 and became VST's first Professor Emeritus.

2

Programs and Curricula*

Most universities in eastern Canada were established by churches, which, in spite of the separation of church and state, still felt they had a custodial role to play in the nurture of the common moral and spiritual values of English-speaking Canadians.[1] Therefore, they devised their college and university curricula to instill into their students sound principles of religion and morality.[2] This Victorian consensus on the balance of faith and reason in higher education, however, had crumbled by the time UBC was established in the twentieth century. As a result there was never a time prior to the 1960s when religion was an integral part of UBC's curriculum.

Religion was removed as part of the core curriculum of the modern American university when President Charles W. Eliot introduced the elective curriculum at Harvard in 1869. This new approach was vigorously opposed by President James McCosh of Princeton, who defended a "prescribed curriculum, compulsory attendance, compulsory religious instruction, strict supervision and discipline, and limited specialization."[3] Unlike McCosh, Eliot did not believe in the unity of knowledge or in the possibility of conveying that unity through a number of compulsory courses. He did not think it was necessary for all educated men and women to know the same things. Indeed, he argued that no standards existed by which to determine whether any body of knowledge was essential for the educated person. Thus, he put an end to compulsory religious

---

* The notes to Chapter 2 are on pp. 66-71.

instruction and chapel attendance at Harvard as well as compulsory courses in moral philosophy and classics.[4] By the end of the nineteenth century, Eliot's view had prevailed, and in the process it transformed the curriculum of all major institutions of higher learning in both the United States and Canada. Consequently, when UBC was established and its founders provided space on campus for the theological colleges, they were simply implementing an understanding of the place of religion in higher education and a pattern of institutional relationships which had been formulated elsewhere prior to the establishment of UBC.

The introduction of religious studies into UBC's curriculum in the 1960s reflected a series of decisions developed elsewhere about its place in the curriculum of the modern university. First, religious studies had to be an elective and not a compulsory core course as it had been in the old nineteenth-century curriculum. Second, when religious studies was given departmental status, it was clear that it would be a subject area in which specialization would be possible through a majors and honours program.[5] Third, its place in the university curriculum was further defined when the first survey of the humanities in Canada was published in 1947 and Watson Kirkconnell indicated that "religion was assumed to lie within the field of humanistic study and experience."[6] Being included in the first major Canadian survey of the humanities defined the position that religious studies would henceforth occupy in the curriculum of the Faculty of Arts. Thus, religious studies at UBC was given the same status as it had received in most other Canadian and American universities.

While this solution satisfied the majority within the university and the theological colleges, there were those in the wider community who found such a solution unacceptable because the Bible and Christianity did not have a central place in the curriculum, because the faculty were not required to be committed Christians who could relate their academic disciplines to the Christian faith, and because chapel services and Christian standards of conduct were not compulsory. These were once the practices of many colleges in the nineteenth century. but they had never been part of the modern university. Indeed, most university administrators had fought hard to remove such restrictions, and their successors never expected to confront them again a century after these battles appeared to have been won. But when the province's "one university" policy and its "anti-sectarian" stance were abandoned in the 1960s, the position that McCosh had so ably defended in the 1870s suddenly reappeared in BC.

As a result, profound differences over the place of religious studies in the undergraduate curriculum and over the assumptions controlling the way it is taught have emerged in the last two decades between the public and private institutions of higher learning in BC. The focus of the conflict has been the question of transfer credit from the private to the public institutions, but the real issue is whether a faculty that has to subscribe to an evangelical statement of faith is free to teach religion in a truly critical and objective manner. In graduate education also there have been tensions between the theological colleges and the university and among the theological colleges themselves. In order to understand the issues involved, therefore, it is necessary to examine the undergraduate and graduate programs in religious studies and theological studies at both public and private institutions in BC.

Teaching Religious Studies at UBC

We begin this chapter with the establishment of the Department of Religious Studies at UBC because it was here that religious studies first received a place in the undergraduate curriculum in BC. The implications of the decision to allow religious studies as an elective subject for specialization within the humanities were not immediately apparent when the Department of Religious Studies was established in 1964. They only became clear as the department began to develop its undergraduate program and to explore the nature of the framework in which it had been placed, a framework common to all departments in the humanities. But since none of the early appointments in religious studies were Canadians with teaching experience in the Arts Faculty of a North American university, many problems in the development of a coherent program were not anticipated.

First, the vast majority of students taking religious studies courses took them as electives. As a result, it would make sense to conceive of the department's undergraduate course offerings as general education courses. What in fact happened was that the curriculum was designed for those who were specializing in religious studies, for it was assumed that they would proceed to graduate work. Thus, the undergraduate curriculum became increasingly controlled by the graduate program, for the primary concern of the department was to ensure that those doing a degree in religious studies at UBC would qualify for entrance into the best graduate schools in the field. Another reason for planning the curriculum around students specializing in religious studies was that it made it possible to develop a coherent program that introduced the subject matter of the field at a relatively simple and general level in the first year and over the following three years proceeded to more complex and particular areas of study that assumed some general background and acquaintance with the fundamental concepts and essential terms in the subject area. What one ended up with by pursuing coherence in this fashion, however, was a highly specialized program for the few and very low enrollments in the third- and fourth-year classes. Furthermore, in focusing on the few who were specializing rather than on the many who were looking for electives, a contradiction, which appeared absurd to those looking at the cost effectiveness of its offerings, was built into the program.

The contradiction becomes even more apparent when one realizes that the number specializing in religious studies was not likely to increase dramatically because a majors or honours degree in this subject area did not qualify students for a vocation. It simply qualified them for graduate studies in the field leading to a masters or doctoral degree which might or might not lead to a teaching position in a college or university. Initially it had been hoped that religious studies would lead in the direction of two other vocational possibilities: the ministry and public school teaching. But shortly after the department was established, it became clear that both of these possibilities were closed.

The theological colleges reacted defensively toward the establishment of departments of religious studies in North America, and in 1956 the ATS issued a "Statement on Pre-Seminary Studies" which declared that those intending to enter the ministry should not specialize in religious studies at the undergraduate level. It recommended that only three courses in religion should be taken in the four-year college span.[7] Criticism of this position appeared in a series of articles published in the *Journal of Bible and Religion.* Ernest C. Colwell, a former dean of the Divinity School at the University of Chicago and president of the Southern California School of Theology at Claremont, attacked the ATS statement, charging that it was this type of attitude that prevented seminaries from becoming true post-graduate institutions.[8] Thus, while most of the graduate and professional schools were advocating greater degrees of specialization at the undergraduate level, the theological schools opposed the trend. As a result, a natural vocational option for majors and honours in religious studies was discouraged, if not actually closed off. Another vocational possibility that had been touted was the teaching of religious studies in the public schools of BC. In the 1960s and early 1970s some experimentation with the teaching of religious studies took place at a few high schools, but it never went beyond the experimental stage because the provincial Department of Education did not establish religious studies as an option in the public school curriculum of BC. Consequently, the faculties of education in the three major provincial universities declined to accept a majors or honours degree in religious studies as a qualification for teacher training; this closed off another vocational outlet. Without these vocational possibilities, therefore, it was inevitable that the number of majors and honours in religious studies would be small.

Between 1945 and 1965 the social sciences began to replace the humanities as the dominant disciplines in the Faculty of Arts. Although history, economics, political science, psychology, sociology, and anthropology never became part of the core curriculum, these disciplines experienced the greatest growth rate in the Faculty of Arts during the post-war years. The humanities, on the other hand, either remained stationary or went into a period of decline. The only disciplines in the humanities that managed to grow were those like English, which offered core courses in the curriculum. Thus, when religious studies was classified as one of the humanities, it was identified with the part of the curriculum that was shrinking rather than expanding.[9]

The Department of Religious Studies had no control over the decisions to classify it as one of the humanities, as an elective, or as a subject area in which specialization would be possible through a majors and honours program. These were decisions made outside the department by such government bodies as the Social Sciences and Humanities Research Council, or university bodies such as the Senate and the Faculty of Arts. On the other hand, the department made decisions regarding the way in which the religious studies program developed, how appointments were determined, and areas of study offered. Thus it is important to consider the type of program that emerged and the thinking behind it.

The Judeo-Christian religious tradition was the initial focus in the department, with Nicholls, Anderson, and Kassis teaching aspects of this tradition. There was nothing particularly surprising about this development because most departments of religious studies in North America were established in exactly the same way.[10] A fourth appointment was made in Buddhism in order to strengthen the non-Christian and non-Western dimensions of the religious studies program at UBC. There was a certain logic behind this fourth appointment, which was made two years after the department was established. Buddhism was one of the most important of the non-Western religions and a major focus in UBC's Department of Asian Studies. Not surprisingly, there was strong support for the appointment in Buddhism from Asian studies. Thus, to focus on Buddhism as the second religious tradition offered by the Department of Religious Studies appeared to be an appropriate direction for the development of the department.[11]

Since this appointment was the first in a tradition other than Christianity, and since it was thought essential that this tradition should be treated in exactly the same way as the Christian tradition, it was decided that the first appointment in Buddhism should be made at the senior level. Consequently, in making this appointment many of the normal conditions were set aside, and Arthur Link was appointed as a tenured full professor, though his publication record did not warrant it. It soon became clear that Link was not particularly interested in undergraduate teaching. As a result, pressure was exerted for a graduate program in Buddhism before the undergraduate program had been firmly established. In 1968, an assistant professor, Shotaro Iida, had to be hired to take care of the undergraduate program and two years later another tenured full professor in Buddhism, Leon Hurvitz, was hired to lay the foundations for a graduate program. As it turned out, all three scholars were specialists in the Mahayana Buddhist tradition and all three were primarily philologists who were interested in translating Buddhist texts. Thus the Theravada Buddhist tradition of South Asia (i.e. South India, Sri Lanka, Burma, Thailand, and Cambodia) was not given the same emphasis.

That the department treated Buddhism differently from the other non-Christian religions is evident in the appointment of junior-level faculty for positions that dealt with other religious traditions. For example, when the Hindu tradition was introduced in 1968, Joseph

Richardson, a former dean of Carey Hall, was appointed as an assistant professor. It was the Vancouver Jewish community that initiated an appointment in Judaism, and they funded a junior-level appointment in this tradition for five years prior to the university assuming financial responsibility. The introduction of the Islamic tradition was not part of the original plan for the department and occurred only because Hanna Kassis shifted the focus of his research and teaching from Old Testament to Islam.[12] The importance of the Bible in the department's offerings, however, was emphasized when Paul Mosca was immediately appointed to fill the Old Testament position.

All appointments made in the department, it should be noted, were specialists in specific religious traditions. Although the need for an appointment in comparative religion or the history of religions was acknowledged, no such appointment was ever made. The undergraduate program that evolved, therefore, placed a heavy emphasis on specialization at the majors and honours level in one of the traditions. Only in the first two years of the program were courses established that spanned more than one religious tradition. While these courses in the first and second years were mandatory for majors and honours, and attracted the greatest number of students taking electives in the department, it was clear that beyond the second year, students were expected to specialize in one of the religious traditions or at most two.

Within six years of the department's establishment, therefore, it was evident that the undergraduate program in religious studies was designed to cover the five major world religions with a special emphasis on Christianity and Buddhism. Moreover, it was clear that it was not thought of as a language department because those specializing in eastern religions were expected to take Sanskrit, Chinese, and Japanese language courses in the Department of Asian Studies. The Department of Classics offered courses in New Testament Greek and medieval Latin for those specializing in the Christian tradition; the languages of scholarship were available in the departments of French, German, Spanish and Italian. Those wishing to specialize in the Old Testament or Islam, however, faced a problem because neither biblical Hebrew nor Arabic were available at UBC. Moreover, none of the existing language departments wanted to handle these languages. More or less by default, therefore, Religious Studies was allowed to develop courses in biblical Hebrew for students in their third and fourth years and in 1989, 25 years after the establishment of the department, permission was finally granted for Religious Studies to offer courses in Arabic at the third- and fourth-year levels for those who wished to specialize in the study of Islam.

When the UBC program in religious studies is compared with similar programs in other Canadian and American institutions, there are some obvious omissions that need to be explained. At the level of area studies there are no courses at UBC in African religions or in the religious development of Latin America. At least part of the reason for these omissions is that these are underdeveloped areas in UBC's general offerings. Religious Studies also offers no courses in the so-called primitive religions, because the Department of Anthropology had a firm lock on this area of study before the Department of Religious Studies was established. Therefore, Religious Studies has had to define itself as a department that deals with the world's living religions and it leaves the areas of myth and ritual in primitive and in native American religions to Anthropology. Likewise, the religions of Greece and Rome are left to the Department of Classics. The department has also paid little attention to new religious movements, cults, sects, and popular religion in North America. The reason for this omission is partly that the focus of its offerings is firmly rooted in the five major religious traditions and partly because much of this material has been left to the Department of Sociology. Recently, however, courses on popular religion in both China and Japan have been introduced into the religious studies curriculum.

As the explanations for the above omissions indicate, Religious Studies is not the only department at UBC with interests in religion.[13] Anthropology, Asian Studies, Classics, and Sociology all have interests in religion. The Department of Philosophy offers courses in the philosophy of religion and medieval philosophy. The Department of Fine Arts has courses in Christian, Buddhist, and Islamic art and the English Department offers a course in the Bible as literature. In all of these departments there are scholars who have published significant works on religion. Thus, it has been necessary for the Department of Religious Studies to define its boundaries in ways that are designed to reduce potential areas of conflict with these other disciplines.

By drawing its boundaries in this way, however, the Department of Religious Studies, as Robert Bellah has pointed out, has failed to control and dominate the entire field of religion within the university in the same way that Economics dominates the study of the economy or Political Science controls the study of politics and political thought.[14] Part of the difficulty is that Religious Studies was a late arrival in the modern university and as a result the larger and more firmly established departments had staked claims to various areas of the study of religion. To recapture this territory, therefore, would have pitted the little guys against the big guys, the newcomers against the oldtimers. If one could have been sure of always occupying the high ground, it might have been possible to play David and Goliath. But, with the lingering Enlightenment tradition of the modern university, which views religion as a negative influence on culture, there has been very little inclination within the Department of Religious Studies at UBC to emulate biblical heros and more of a tendency to look for allies in the cultural politics of academia.

The retrenchment and financial difficulties experienced by educational institutions in BC during the 1980s have had the effect of imposing quite a different conception of the equality of the religious traditions on the Department of Religious Studies. Each of the traditions, with the exception of Hinduism, was represented by one full-time appointment. The initial reaction to the loss of so many positions in the department was a sense of dismemberment and the fear that the department was about to disappear by a process of attrition. More recently, however, retrenchment has come to be seen in a more positive light as a process that has eliminated many past mistakes in the development and conception of the program in religious studies. A new opportunity has arisen to rethink the structure of the program and to lay new foundations for the development of an undergraduate program that deals more constructively with the context in which religious studies finds itself as an elective in the humanities with limited vocational outlets. At the same time, this rethinking has the potential to offer both specialists and non-specialists many opportunities in area studies, cultural studies, ethnic studies, and the functions of religion in a multicultural society.

At present, the Department of Religious Studies at UBC offers seven areas of concentration for major and honours undergraduate degree programs: Asian religions, Christianity (post-biblical), Hebrew Bible and the Ancient Near East, Islamic studies, Judaic studies, Near Eastern languages and literature, and New Testament. The description of the introductory course on the major religions of the world provides a good summary of the approach adopted by the department: "The focus will be on the origins and representative texts along with some historical development and current experience of each religion. Included will be introductory lectures on the nature and definition of religion with a sampling of some of the theories regarding the origins of religion."[15] The course deals with the various elements that make up religious life, such as myth, ritual, symbol, authoritative writings and practices, ethics, the idea of the holy, and the expressions of these elements in art and music. The advanced course on the concepts and methods in the study of religion required of all majors and honours students takes a broad eclectic approach covering "the various theoretical frameworks and methodologies presently used in the scientific study of religion."[16] The department also offers MA programs in biblical studies, Christian thought and institutions, the history of religions, Islamic studies, Judaic studies, and the religions of South and East Asia.[17]

In his 1972 survey of religious study departments in fourteen hundred colleges and universities in the United States and Canada, Claude Welch noted that "there seems to be a definite correlation between the academic quality of an educational institution and the likelihood of its having a program of religious studies."[18] With their more market-driven curricula, however, the other public universities and community colleges in BC have manifested very little embarrassment over the fact that they do not possess either departments of religious studies or organized programs in the field.[19] There is no evidence to suggest that their failure to create departments of religious studies has been based on careful studies of the problems and difficulties that developed at UBC. But the decision of the provincial Department of Education not to offer religious studies in the public schools and the relatively low enrollments that have resulted from a lack of vocational outlets appears to have been sufficient reason for the failure of the other public institutions in the province to offer organized programs of religious studies. On occasion, individual courses in religious studies have been offered in these institutions when enrollments were sufficiently high to justify them. But in periods of budget restraint, these courses have usually been the first to be cut. Indeed, the only reason the community colleges have for offering such courses is that they provide the possibility of transfer credit to UBC. Without this possibility, it appears unlikely that any of the community colleges would offer religious studies courses even on an occasional basis. Hence, at the present time, there is little reason to anticipate any radical change on this question in the other public institutions and for the foreseeable future it is likely that UBC will be the only public university in the province to offer a full program in religious studies.

Theological Studies at Bible Colleges and Trinity Western University

When the academic revolution in higher education occurred in North America during the last three decades of the nineteenth century, the Christian colleges that attempted to retain the old patterns and assumptions collapsed in disarray.[20] Scottish Common Sense assumptions in philosophy and confessional stances in theology gave way to idealistic, developmental, and historicist conceptions of higher education. The older institutions had existed to form character rather than to transmit knowledge. Hence the emphasis in the older institutions was on guidance, protection, and shepherding of students rather than on specialization, expertise, and research. The curricula of the new universities were shaped by secular and pluralistic values rather than Christianity, and the primary commitment of these new institutions was to scientific truth and pragmatic usefulness. In the face of this revolutionary transformation, therefore, those who had serious doubts about the impact of this new institution on Christian civilization were forced to the sidelines of the educational enterprise. Since they opposed the secularism and pluralism of the new universities and saw these as dangerous threats to the religious faith of future generations, they needed alternative educational institutions to train their leadership. Initially, the institution to which conservative Protestants turned was the bible college.

The two main figures in the establishment of the bible colleges as institutions of higher education were Albert B. Simpson and Dwight L. Moody.[21] Simpson (1843-1919) was a Canadian Presbyterian from Bayview, Prince Edward Island. In 1865 he graduated from Knox College, Toronto and held pastorates in Hamilton, Ontario, Louisville, Kentucky, and Thirteenth Street Presbyterian Church in New York City. In 1881 he resigned from the Thirteenth Street Church and began independent evangelistic work which eventually resulted in the formation of a new denomination, the Christian and Missionary Alliance. In his evangelistic work, Simpson discovered that many young people who were offering themselves for missionary service did not have the advantages of a good secular education and for a variety of reasons were not in a position to spend seven years in college and seminary in order to qualify as missionaries. Therefore, in 1883 Simpson established the first bible college in North America in New York City.[22] As a result of his evangelistic work Dwight L. Moody arrived at similar conclusions in 1886 when he laid the foundations for the Moody Bible Institute in Chicago, designed to provide training for men and women who wished to work full time in Christian mission work and social service, but not as clergy.

In all cases, those who established bible colleges were clear that they were not establishing theological colleges, which were seen as professional schools for the clergy, requiring college degrees for admission. Their intention was to train those who did not have college degrees for missionary work and evangelistic service. As a result, there was no attempt to affiliate these institutions with universities or to seek degree-granting powers. Three bible colleges were founded in Canada prior to the establishment of the Toronto Bible Training School in 1894. The first was the Mission Training School at Niagara Falls, which was established in 1885. The second was the Christian Institute, which was established in Toronto by Alfred Sandham, and the third was the Toronto Missionary Training School, founded by John Salmon in 1893. All of these schools had close connections with Simpson's Christian and Missionary Alliance church. Believing that schools sponsored by this new denomination could not properly represent the broader conservative evangelical community in Toronto, Elmore Harris of Walmer Road Baptist Church established the Toronto Bible Training School in 1894. It was dominated by Baptists and Presbyterians, but also had Methodists and Anglicans among its early leaders and, unlike most other bible colleges in Canada, was a lay training institute for the Canadian mainline Protestant denominations until well into the twentieth century.[23]

Like the theological colleges, the Toronto Bible Training School adopted a three-year program that focused on the devotional rather than the critical study of the Bible and provided courses in "all the subjects that are found in the curriculum of the average theological seminary."[24] Although it offered a full theological curriculum, the Toronto Bible Training School was clear about its role as "a trainer of laypeople" which, in its view, "did not overlap or interfere with that of the denominational [theological] colleges." Using a military analogy, principal John McNicol saw the theological colleges as training facilities for the officers of God's army and the bible colleges as the training centre for the rank and file of that army.[25] The fact that many of the newer and smaller denominations in Canada were prepared to ordain graduates of the bible colleges, however, meant that about 10 percent of the Toronto Bible Training School's graduates did eventually end up in the ministry. This trend became more marked after the fundamentalist-modernist controversy began and two-party Protestantism emerged in Canada during the 1920s and 1930s.

As indicated in the first chapter, the Vancouver Bible College was the second major bible college in Canada; it served the conservative evangelical Protestant community in BC until the 1950s. By the time it closed its doors, a number of smaller denominations had either established their own bible colleges or were thinking about opening such schools. As a result, there are now five major bible colleges in BC accredited by the Association of Canadian Bible Colleges and a half dozen others which are not accredited or empowered to grant theological degrees such as the BTh or the BRE.

Because the academic revolution of the final decades of the nineteenth century had removed the Bible from the undergraduate curriculum, the main focus of the bible college curriculum was to put the Bible back into the curriculum.[26] Rejecting both the idea that serious biblical study had to be done in the original languages and by the methods of interpretation adopted by the liberal theological seminaries, the bible colleges concentrated on the study of the Bible in English from a confessional or devotional stance.[27] In many cases, the method adopted was a synthetic approach based on the dispensational theology of the Scofield Reference Bible. Once one had mastered the panoramic view of the Bible offered by dispensationalism, it was then possible to move on to biblical doctrines and theology, biblical characters, single books, great chapters, key words, biblical prophecy, and biblical geography. The ultimate object of these courses was to provide the student with the ability to come up instantly with a Bible verse to cover every possible occasion. These courses, therefore, led very naturally into courses in personal evangelism, preaching, and Christian education. The General Bible Course was the centrepiece of the bible college curriculum. But since the schools were training lay church workers and foreign missionaries, other courses were usually available in church music, Christian education, and the history and principles of Christian missions.

Furthermore, since many of the early bible colleges were modeled on the normal schools and vocational institutes that were being established at roughly the same time, another important dimension of these schools was the practical training they demanded of all their students. This practical work involved them in a variety of work assignments such as Sunday School teaching, advising youth groups, assisting in rescue missions, settlement houses, and city missions, distributing tracts door-to-door, and visiting in prisons, asylums, hospitals, and institutions for the elderly. Those training for foreign missions worked with immigrant groups. This part of the program was based on the theory that one learns by doing. In addition, the problems encountered provided plenty of opportunities for reflection and for questions when the students returned to the classroom.

Though many find it hard to associate the work of the bible colleges in BC with what is normally thought of as higher education, it must be remembered that it was these institutions that enabled the conservative evangelical Protestant community both in BC and elsewhere to survive over the past century and to train a vigorous core of leaders for their churches and overseas mission fields. Moreover, it is these institutions that laid the foundations for the new ventures in higher education, like Trinity Western University, which have been sponsored and supported by the evangelical churches in BC. Indeed, it is not possible to understand the distinctive features of Trinity Western unless its curriculum is seen in relation to the type of curriculum first developed in the bible colleges.

The relationship between Trinity Western and the bible colleges becomes apparent especially in the curriculum of its Department of Religious Studies in the Faculty of Arts and Religious Studies, where 24 of the 54 courses offered by the division are on the Bible (12 on the Old Testament and 12 on the New Testament). This emphasis stands in marked contrast to the 44 courses in religious studies at UBC, where only five courses are on the Bible. Moreover, while all of the Bible courses offered in religious studies at UBC are electives, of the 12 semester hours in religious studies at Trinity Western required for graduation in all fields, nine must be in Bible. These requirements, of course, are not surprising in a school of which the first article of the statement of faith is: "We believe the Scriptures, both Old and New Testaments, to be the inspired Word of God, without error in the original writings, the complete revelation of His will for the salvation of men, and the divine and final authority for all Christian faith and life."[28] Also, these requirements should not be surprising in a school where students must sign a form agreeing to abide by the community standards of Trinity Western University, which are based on "biblical principles" and specifically prohibit "swearing or the use of profane language," "abortion," "involvement in the occult," and "sexual sins" such as "premarital sex, adultery, and homosexual behaviour," "the use of alcoholic beverages, gambling, tobacco in any form, marijuana and drugs for non-medical purposes," and "social dancing."[29]

Both the statement of faith and the community standards covenant are common in other North American conservative evangelical Protestant universities in the Association of Christian Colleges. The emphasis on the study of the Bible as part of the core curriculum is also a standard feature of these institutions. What distinguishes Trinity Western from the bible colleges is that while the majority of the courses are based on the English Bible, as they are at UBC, courses are also offered in biblical Hebrew and New Testament Greek for those who wish to do advanced biblical study in the original languages. That it offers courses on Christian missions and cross-cultural communication, however, shows that the conception of the nature and purpose of the religious studies program at Trinity Western is to offer theological studies, much as do the bible colleges.

The most important difference between the religious studies programs at UBC and Trinity Western is that at Trinity Western there is only one course in World Religions and no courses in Buddhism, Hinduism, Judaism, or Islam. At UBC, on the other hand, courses in these religious traditions account for half of the department's undergraduate offerings. In other words, the emphasis of the religious studies program at Trinity Western is almost exclusively on Christianity, whereas at UBC only four of the 39 courses are exclusively concerned with post-biblical Christianity and only one of these courses is currently offered every year. These differences in emphasis, which are embodied in the religious studies curricula of Trinity Western University and UBC, would be of only passing interest as distinguishing features of the respective approaches to religious studies at a public non-sectarian institution and a private Christian institution, were it not for the fact that UBC has refused to offer any transfer credit in religious studies for courses taken at Trinity Western University. This refusal has been the source of considerable tension and conflict between the two institutions and therefore some analysis of the issue is required.

The policy of refusing transfer credit to Trinity Western students in the Religious Studies field became an issue in the 1980s when Kenneth R. Davis, the vice-president and dean of Academic Affairs at Trinity Western University, wrote to Dr. Peter Remnant, the associate dean of Arts at UBC, complaining that UBC was rejecting Trinity Western's religious studies courses on the basis of the "requirement that Trinity Western faculty give assent to a statement of religious faith." Davis argued that UBC would stand "virtually alone institutionally in North America in holding to this narrow interpretation of scholarship." Furthermore, "UBC would be the only university in Canada to reject our religious studies credits on the basis of our being a Christian university." This position, Davis continued, was a misinterpretation of "the non-sectarian intent of the Universities Act which is primarily designed to ensure openness and to avoid the establishment of one or any religion in the public institutions. It was never intended to become judgemental of the academic qualifications of non-public universities nor to prohibit transfer credit between public and private institutions." Consequently, Davis urged that "these inappropriate and subjective criteria be reviewed by the Faculty of Arts," and if this failed to alter the policy on the matter, he stated that "we hereby lodge an official appeal to the Senate of UBC to review and invalidate the negative criteria employed by the Department of Religious Studies in its assessment of Trinity Western College's courses."[30]

In his reply to Davis, Remnant ignored the request for reference of this question to the Faculty of Arts and the UBC Senate. He confined his remarks exclusively to clarifying UBC's position on transfer credit for courses in religious studies. He argued that when UBC accepted courses from other institutions, in effect it adopted those courses as its own. Therefore, it had to assure itself that the material in these courses had been presented with non-sectarian objectivity. Because of its commitments to evangelical Christian doctrine, however, it was clear that Trinity Western University opposed the spirit of non-sectarian objectivity. As a result, UBC could not grant transfer credit for Trinity Western's courses in religious studies without violating the Universities Act. This decision, Remnant concluded, applied not only to courses given at Trinity Western University, but also to courses given at UBC's affiliated theological colleges.[31] Davis, of course, wanted more than a clarification of UBC's position. He wanted the position changed. Hence, it did not take long before further representations were made to Daniel R. Birch, the acting vice-president academic at UBC, who referred the matter to Dean Robert M. Will of the Faculty of Arts.

In his reply, Will made it clear that in refusing transfer credit to Trinity Western's religious studies courses, "the focus has not been on individual courses, on whether or not they were being taught in an appropriate manner and at an appropriate level, but on these courses as a class of offerings . . . for which we feel a doctrinal statement has implications." Will conceded that university faculty members have biases, but the university expects its faculty to keep these under control or they will be "called" by university administrators who have a responsibility to see that the faculty do not allow their biases to distort their vision either in their research or teaching. "The hallmark of a liberal education," Will continued, "is a learning environment that encourages inquiry, the open-ended pursuit of knowledge, and even doubt. Yet this is impossible if a particular approach or perspective to knowledge is treated as an absolute and becomes institutionalized in a creed, statement of belief, etc." Therefore, he concluded, "people who reject the non-sectarian (read humanistic) university follow at their own expense an alternative path. Can they have it both ways? This seems to be what they are asking in expecting unquestioned transfer credit in courses in Religious Studies."[32]

At the moment this is where the issue stands. Moreover, for the foreseeable future it appears as if UBC's policy will remain unchanged because Trinity Western is the only private sectarian university with a religious studies program and UBC is the only public university with a religious studies program. Besides, UBC's policy creates no difficulties for its affiliated theological colleges because they do not offer undergraduate degrees. Consequently, there is very little pressure on UBC to reconsider its policy.

In September 1988, when it was necessary for UBC to hire someone on extremely short notice to teach a course in New Testament, it appeared as if this policy might become slightly unravelled because the only qualified person who was available to teach the course was Craig Evans, chair of the Religious Studies Division at Trinity Western University. Evans was one of the Trinity Western faculty who had taken particular exception to UBC's refusal of transfer credit to Trinity Western's religious studies courses and his sharply worded comments on this policy had accompanied Davis's letter to Remnant.[33] The question that arose was that if Evans's courses at Trinity Western were not acceptable for transfer credit at UBC, then how could his courses taught at UBC be eligible for credit? For Will there was no contradiction here, for when Evans was teaching at Trinity Western he had to comply with their conditions of appointment. At UBC, however, his teaching was under the conditions of appointment at UBC, which made no faith demands of him whatsoever. Provided he was qualified and fulfilled his contractual duties as laid down by UBC, the university had no reservations about hiring him or granting credit for courses taught at UBC. Thus, his appointment at UBC, far from being an embarrassment, was seen as a confirmation of the fact that the refusal of transfer credit was never directed at individual instructors or their qualifications but rather at the sectarian requirements of an institution.

For many years similar arrangements have been made with faculty members from the affiliated colleges who were hired to teach courses when various members of the Department of Religious Studies were on leave. In these cases the policy was exactly the same as the one applied to Trinity Western University. UBC will not give transfer credit for courses taken in the theological colleges, but it has no objection to faculty from the theological colleges teaching UBC courses. To focus on such a minute point of policy may seem unwarranted, but these distinctions are designed to safeguard the integrity of UBC's religious studies program and it is anticipated that the application of such distinctions will be necessary in the further development of the graduate program in the field of religion.

Graduate Theological Studies

Graduate studies in religion developed first in the theological colleges because following the academic revolution in higher education, the study of religion was confined to these professional schools.[34] Prior to the 1960s, therefore, most graduate programs in religion focused exclusively on Christianity. Since the establishment of departments of religious studies in the modern secular universities, this focus and emphasis has started to change. But in order to understand the development of graduate studies in religion, it is essential to begin by examining the emergence of the theological colleges, the nature of their curriculum, and the contribution that these institutions have made to graduate studies in BC.

Exactly when theological colleges emerged in Canada is not exactly known because no historian of Canadian theological education has defined a theological college or properly distinguished it from the former apprenticeship system of training.[35] In the United States, Robert Wood Lynn has developed a four-part definition of the theological college which has been widely accepted by historians working in this area. The four essential characteristics of a theological college as outlined by Lynn are: "a three year academic programme, a resident faculty of three or more, an institution independent of the colleges [or universities] and designed for the post-collegiate [or post-baccalaureate] training of clergy."[36] Andover Seminary, established in 1808, was the first North American theological college possessing these characteristics; it was followed four years later by Princeton Theological Seminary. Because they were the first to be established, these two seminaries did a considerable amount of experimenting with curriculum before they both adopted the four-fold program of Bible, historical and systematic theology, church history, and practical theology that has formed the core curriculum of the Protestant theological colleges up to our own time.

If this definition of a theological college is accepted, the next question is, when did this type of a school emerge in Canada? It is very difficult to get a satisfactory answer from the currently available literature but it appears that Knox College, Toronto, was the first to become a separate theological college, partly because the Free Church, following the Disruption, had to create new colleges in which to train its clergy in Scotland, and partly because in Canada they did not want to have anything to do with Queen's, which was an Auld Kirk institution. Thus, the Free Church Presbyterians in Canada were the first to form a separate theological college in 1844. Yet it was not until 1861 that there was more than one individual who devoted his full time to teaching in this college. After the union of the Free Church and the United Presbyterian Church in 1861 and the amalgamation of the United Presbyterian Divinity Hall in London, Ontario, with Knox, there were finally three full-time professors: Michael Willis in theology, William Caven in biblical exegesis, and J.J. Proudfoot in homiletics, pastoral theology, and church government. While the Congregationalists were the first to require a BA degree from McGill as a prerequisite for theology in 1876, and Presbyterian College, Halifax, made an arts degree a prerequisite for theology two years later, Knox remained ambivalent on this question until the 1880s because it had a preparatory program for those without BAs. Again, the Congregationalists appear to have been the first to adopt the four fold curriculum in 1855. The Presbyterians had adopted a similar program by the 1860s.[37] It was not until 1881, however, that Knox received degree-granting powers, and it was not until 1889 that the Anglican colleges were allowed to grant BD and DD degrees. It seems possible, therefore, to conclude that theological colleges, in Lynn's sense of the term, began to emerge in most of the Canadian mainline Protestant denominations by the 1880s.

The curriculum of these Protestant schools was also standardized by the 1880s; it followed the four-fold program of Bible, theology, church history, and practical theology that had been developed in Europe and the United States.[38] Normally this curriculum involved three years of Old Testament (with a brief introduction to archaeology and Near Eastern religions), three years of New Testament, three years of theology (which included philosophy of religion, historical theology, and the study of modern systematic theologians), three years of church history (early and medieval in the first year, the Reformation in the second, and modern in the third year), and three years of practical theology (which included Christian education, Christian ethics, pastoral counselling, homiletics, elocution, the history of Christian worship and hymnody, as well as church government). Those who completed this program received a diploma in theology which qualified them for ordination. Those with a first-class average, however, were allowed to proceed, either in the course of the three-year program or by taking an extra year, to the BD. Although this degree was the first professional degree, not more than 30 percent of those taking theological training bothered to take it and those who did usually intended to go on to graduate studies, for the BD was an essential requirement for entrance into all higher degrees in the field. This program, with minor variations, was standard in most Protestant theological colleges in Canada from the 1880s through to the 1960s.

This pattern of theological education was transferred from central Canada to BC, as we have seen in the first chapter. All the colleges were small, but the aspirations of the founders were shaped by the curricula for educating clergy that existed in the colleges of their respective denominations in central Canada. Bible, systematic theology, church history, and practical theology formed the substance of the curriculum in each of the schools. In the Methodist and Presbyterian traditions the major emphasis in practical theology was on homiletics and elocution, with some attention given to church music and pastoral visiting. Among the Anglicans more emphasis was placed on liturgics and spiritual disciplines. Thus, the programs in theological colleges in BC were defined elsewhere and imported.

The creation of the Vancouver School of Theology in 1971 coincided with a period of discussion and debate over the content of theological education in North America. The focus of the debate was the appropriate design of a curriculum for the education of clergy. The primary lines of cleavage ran between the academic fields of Bible, theology, and church history, and the practical fields of Christian education, pastoral counselling, homiletics, church management, and polity. Prior to World War II, the emphasis in theological colleges in North America had been on academic education. It was assumed that students for the clergy would enter the college with broad experience in the life of their particular denomination and that the example of their professors, themselves successful parish priests or congregational ministers, would provide the necessary influences that would form them into effective practitioners of ministry. The role of the theological college, then, was to focus on intellectual preparation in the academic disciplines, with some attention paid to communicating that knowledge in the pulpit, in the Bible class, and in pastoral conversation. Much of the pastoral formation, however, was left to informal processes within the college community or to other agencies of the church. Following World War II, funding for studies, institutes, and chairs in the practical disciplines, especially pastoral psychology and counselling, brought an increasing demand for space for practical courses in the curriculum. Samuel Blizzard's studies of what clergy actually did in the 1950s heightened the demands from sponsoring churches and college alumni for a better balance in theological education between the academic and the practical, a balance that reflected the practice of the profession.[39] The ATS, with funding from several large foundations in the United States, conducted a series of studies on education for ministry between the 1950s and the 1980s that documented the confusion in expectations and programs among the theological colleges and their sponsoring constituencies.[40]

In a feasibility study done for a Joint Committee of the Anglican and United colleges in Vancouver in 1969, Charles Taylor reviewed the kinds of people interested in studying religion and the types of institutions best suited to them. He drew a clear line of separation between religious studies and theological studies. The university clearly served those interested in "the scientific study of religions." While Taylor appeared sympathetic to the expressed desire of the theological colleges to build bridges with the university in the study of religion, he concluded that this should not deflect them from their primary purpose of providing education for people preparing for, or engaged in, some form of ministry in the churches. Those interested in teaching in a university or theological college should be sent elsewhere, until the proposed ecumenical centre of theological studies developed sufficient resources for advanced study. Taylor concluded that the Anglicans and Uniteds should join in creating a centre of theological studies that would be professional in focus, practical in emphasis, and innovative in curriculum to meet the needs of a changing church and world.[41]

The Vancouver School of Theology was founded in 1971; James P. Martin was called from Union Seminary in Richmond, Virginia, to be principal in 1972. The founders gave Martin a mandate to gather a new faculty and design a new program for theological education. In his inaugural address, Martin made it clear that the focus of the new program would be theological studies in the service of the ecumenical commitments of the sponsoring mainline denominations. He argued that the identity and credibility of the church in the modern world depended on the faith that the church had in the crucified and resurrected Christ. This was the first principle of Christian theology and hence the guiding principle for a school devoted to education for ministry. Training for professional ministry, theological studies, ecumenical relations, and mission were the tasks that the church had assigned to the school. By performing these functions, the school prepared students to live in freedom and service to "the Word of the Cross" in and through the church. At the same time, these activities represented a public demonstration and profession of Christian humanism in the context of the wider humanism of the community of learning at the university.[42]

The influence of Union Seminary in the evolution of VST's program philosophy was extensive. Using Union's innovative competence curriculum more as inspiration than model, VST initiated its own competence curriculum in 1974.[43] It was designed specifically to overcome many of the tensions between the academic and practical disciplines and to address the concerns from the sponsoring denominations for more effective professional education. In a master competence document developed by the VST Senate, five areas of competence expected of a pastor-theologian were listed:

- competence in ministering to and with congregations as preacher, teacher, and liturgist;

- competence in leadership in organizational life and work in the congregation and community;

- competence in ministering in mission to the world;

- competence in ministering to individual persons; and

- competence in developing the priest's/minister's own personal resources.

In each of the five areas, four dimensions of competence were identified: skills, knowledge, faith, and maturity.

The program acknowledged that many people had learned much before they embarked on study at VST. A locating process was established to enable faculty and students to discern what skills and knowledge had been developed prior to enrolment at VST. Further, the design recognized that some areas of competence were best left to further life experience and continuing education. The former was designated Level 1 and the latter Level 4. Levels 2 and 3 were served by the MDiv program. Level 2 consisted of intensive study in the basic theological disciplines and Level 3 provided specialized training for ministry that sharpened theological awareness and increased competence in various forms of professional ministry. Throughout the program, learning how to reflect theologically on experience was stressed in order to develop competence in faith and maturity.

Three divisions — Bible, History/Theology, and Theology and Practice of Ministry — were created to develop the skills and knowledge deemed necessary to be a competent pastor-theologian. Each division established a series of competencies appropriate to the represented disciplines that had to be proven prior to an examination that tested students' ability to integrate what they had learned. The evaluation system was designed to encourage cooperation rather than competition among students. Four levels of competence were established: not yet approved, approved, very good, and exceptional. In the integrating examination, the faculty assessed the readiness of the student to enter Level 3 of the program which consisted of field education in a church, community, or hospital setting, pastoral studies seminars, electives, and a thesis on ministry. Some changes took place in the greater prominence given to mission in the curriculum, in the language used to describe the curriculum, and in the organization of its various elements in the 1980s, but the fundamental structure remained intact.[44] The principles around which the entire curriculum was designed were competence in ministry and integration of disciplines.

The MDiv program at VST was a radical break with the pattern in other theological colleges in Canada. Its professional focus on the pastor-theologian in the church in mission and its experience-based model of learning made it unique in Canada. Feedback from graduates in two ATS self-study documents indicated general satisfaction with the program among those who went into parish ministry or church-related work.[45] The unusual curriculum design and categories for evaluation did create problems for those wishing to pursue graduate studies in theology at other institutions, but it also opened new possibilities for providing education for ministry.

In 1985, VST agreed to join with the British Columbia Conference of the United Church of Canada, the Diocese of Caledonia of the Anglican Church of Canada, and the Charles Cook School of the Presbyterian Church (USA) to form the Native Ministries Consortium. In 1987, VST agreed to offer a MDiv degree by extension for persons working primarily with native peoples. The curriculum developed incorporated all the competencies and requirements of the residential degree, but took native traditions and community contexts seriously.[46]

The Vancouver School of Theology offers three other degree programs, a Master of Theological Studies and a Master of Pastoral

Studies related to its mandate in lay education, and a Master of Theology related to its mandate in continuing education. The former are two-year residential degrees using the course offerings in the MDiv program, the former with a focus on academic studies and the latter with a focus on field education in the practical disciplines of societal ministries, Christian education, and pastoral care. The latter is primarily a non-residential degree for MDiv graduates, with courses offered at summer school by visiting faculty from around the world and a thesis written under the direction of a member of the VST faculty. Since 1994, under the initial direction of Dr. Phillips, VST has also offered credit courses to some of those who are not resident in the school. Distance learning programs are carried to students in parts of the lower mainland and Victoria, and serve registered students as well as others who wish to audit the courses. Courses towards the Master of Theological Studies, the Master of Pastoral Studies, and the Master of Divinity degrees are offered in this way.

The other major initiative in BC in program and curricula on this level came from Regent College, founded in 1968 on the UBC campus by a group of Plymouth Brethren businessmen and educators, with James M. Houston as principal. Houston, a prominent British Brethren who had been lecturer in geography and fellow of Hertford College, Oxford, insisted that the new school be close to, if not affiliated with, the university, that it be a graduate school, and that it be transdenominational. It would differ from both bible colleges and theological seminaries. The former were designed for those without university degrees, while the latter served those destined for ordained ministry. In keeping with the Brethren tradition, Regent sought not to distinguish between clergy and laity in its programs. The college would emphasize interdisciplinary studies and interpret the modern world from an evangelical Christian perspective. Initial plans included a one-year course for university graduates in business or professional careers who wanted a theological foundation for their secular work, a masters program for those wishing to engage in extended biblical and theological studies, and research support and facilities leading eventually to a doctoral program.[47]

The first program designed was the Diploma in Christian Studies, designed "to assist university and college graduates in formulating a world view integrating their professional training and their Christian faith."[48] It required a year of full-time study consisting of 15 units or 30 credit hours in the traditional disciplines of Bible, theology, and church history, and a course in cross-disciplinary studies. The first degree program was the Master of Christian Studies. It built on the diploma and added another 30 credit hours consisting of Bible, theology, church history, interdisciplinary study, and a thesis that attempted to understand the relationship between the Christian faith and an area of study outside the bounds of the traditional theological curriculum. Later, a Master of Theological Studies degree was added, also a two-year, 60 credit-hour program, which allowed for special concentration in one of the disciplines represented in the curriculum. In the MCS, 15 credit hours were allocated to thesis preparation, while in the MTS the same time was spent in courses and examinations in the area of concentration.

The MDiv degree was established in 1979. Pressure had been building over the decade to provide professional education through a MDiv program, especially from the Baptist Union of Western Canada and parachurch organizations such as Inter-Varsity Christian Fellowship, Young Life of Canada and Youth For Christ.[49] Regent and Carey Hall, the Baptist college at UBC, agreed to cooperate in offering the degree, with Regent providing the core academic courses and Carey providing the faculty and courses in applied theology. A joint library project was launched to provide the required resources for full ATS accreditation. The curriculum incorporated the one-year diploma, with its interdisciplinary focus, but placed special emphasis on communication through preaching, teaching, and counselling. The 90 credit hours required for the MDiv consisted of 12 in Bible, 15 in theology and ethics, six in church history, six in interdisciplinary studies, 15 in applied theology, and 21 hours of electives. Concentrations in pastoral ministry, biblical studies, biblical languages, theology, evangelism, and urban studies were possible by taking 15 of the 21 hours of electives in the area of specialization.

Regent College also created a MTh degree program that required an additional 30 credit hours to the MDiv and an additional 60 credit hours to the MTS or the MCS. The focus of the degree is on academic research and thesis writing in one of the disciplines offered in the curriculum. A Chinese Studies Program, established in 1985 and staffed by a full-time director since 1989, seeks to promote research on the relationship between Christianity and Chinese culture. It organizes conferences on "strategic issues relevant to the

Chinese Church" and arranges special courses in the Regent curriculum. A Chinese Studies concentration is available in the MTS and the MCS programs.[50]

Program design and balance are areas of ongoing tension within the Regent College community. On one side is the vision of its Plymouth Brethren founders of a graduate institute or centre of theological studies that offers an opportunity for Christians from all walks of life to engage in a serious study of the bearing of their faith on the social and cultural issues of their time. Ranged against this is the more recent effort, in response to student and constituency pressure, to provide degree programs for professional ministry. Programs to address both concerns are offered, but which one deserves and gets priority remains a point of contention.

The Vancouver School of Theology and Regent are not the only institutions offering theological studies at the graduate level in BC. The Associated Canadian Theological Schools is a consortium of believers' church seminaries representing the Baptist General Conference of Canada, the Evangelical Free Church of Canada, and the Fellowship of Evangelical Baptist Churches of Canada, formed in 1988 and affiliated with Trinity Western University. The denominations are small, claiming fewer than 700 churches across Canada among the three of them. ACTS requires subscription to a statement of faith that expresses the core of believers' church theology, i.e., the need for new birth, adult baptism, local church autonomy, and the inerrancy of Scripture. The consortium offers five graduate theological degrees: a three-year MDiv and a two-year MTS for those with undergraduate degrees; a MTS in counselling, with the option of gaining CAPE (Canadian Association for Pastoral Education) certification; a MRE; and a Master of Ministry for pastors, missionaries, and church leaders with bible college training and at least three years of experience in ministry. All the programs follow a course model with an emphasis on biblical studies and evangelism. The consortium is an associate member of ATS.[51]

In 1989, informal preliminary discussions among representatives of VST, Regent, Trinity Western University, and the Department of Religious Studies at UBC were held to explore the possibility of pooling resources to offer doctoral programs. There was a strong desire among the faculty at all four institutions to work cooperatively in establishing doctoral programs in religious and theological studies in British Columbia. Institutional support, however, was less than enthusiastic. Regent and Trinity Western seemed keen. The Vancouver School of Theology was hesitant because of the time, effort, and funding going into the recently launched Native Ministries Degree Program. UBC expressed willingness to explore the possibility of a doctoral program in some areas of religious studies, but did not show much initiative. Informal discussions have continued since 1989 and the current generation of leaders at VST, Regent, UBC's Department of Religious Studies, and UBC's Faculty of Graduate Studies seem interested in pursuing the possibility of a doctoral program again. It is clear, however, that none of the institutions on its own can offer graduate study at the doctoral level.

Institutions and programs of religious and theological studies in BC, then, are isolated from one another. There is no transfer of credit from the institutions offering theological studies to the one offering religious studies, though courses in religious studies can be transferred the other way by special arrangement. Regent College and VST offer mutual transfer of courses and credit, but differences in theological orientation mean that students seldom use this option. The Department of Religious Studies at UBC does not accept transfer credit for courses at Trinity Western, while theological stance and the lack of ATS accreditation make transfer credits between Trinity Western's affiliated theological colleges and Regent or VST difficult. It is among the faculties of these institutions, especially in their research and membership in learned societies, that some interchange does take place. To complete the survey of religious and theological studies in BC, it is necessary to determine who has been teaching the programs, what their research interests have been, and whether there are any signs of closer relations developing among the institutions.

Notes

1 A table indicating the religious origins of Canadian universities, the dates of their founding, and their present status is contained in Wilson Woodside, *The University Question: Who Should Go? Who Should Pay?* (Toronto: Ryerson, 1958), 15-16.

2 A.B. McKillop, *A Disciplined Intelligence: Critical Inquiry and Canadian Thought in the Victorian Era* (Montreal: McGill-Queen's University Press, 1979), 1-21.

3 See Frederick Rudolph, *The American College and University: A History* (New York: Vintage, 1962), 298, and Laurence R. Veysey, *The Emergence of the American University* (Chicago: University of Chicago Press, 1965), 1-56. See also James McCosh, *Religion in a College: What Place It Should Have* (New York, 1886), and J. David Hoeveler, Jr., *James McCosh and the Scottish Intellectual Tradition: From Glasgow to Princeton* (Princeton: Princeton University Press, 1981), 233-39 and 252-54. The statements of Eliot and McCosh on this question are contained in *American Higher Education: A Documentary History,* vol. 2, ed. Richard Hofstadter and Wilson Smith (Chicago: University of Chicago Press, 1961), 697-747. The most important single essay on these developments is Richard Hofstadter, "The Revolution in Higher Education," in *Paths Of American Thought*, ed. Arthur M. Schlesinger, Jr. and Morton White (Boston: Houghton Mifflin, 1963), 269-89.

4 It was not until 1886 that Harvard finally abandoned compulsory chapel attendance. Earlier, in 1876, Johns Hopkins University abandoned invocational prayers at its opening ceremonies. UBC, however, still opens its graduation ceremonies with prayer and it arranges for a Baccalaureate Service just prior to graduation for the family and friends of those who are graduating. While these are interesting survivals from another era, this is not the place to examine the public rituals of the University of British Columbia.

5 There were other ways of handling religious studies that had been discussed prior to the establishment of the department at UBC. For example, see Huston Smith, "The Interdepartmental Approach to Religious Studies: An Account of the Program at Washington University," *Journal of Higher Education*, 31, 2 (February 1960): 61-68. As Claude Welch has pointed out, however, the vast majority of public institutions offering full programs in religious studies have placed these programs in either separate departments (60 percent) or combined departments such as Philosophy and Religion (32 percent). See Claude Welch, *Religion in the Undergraduate Curriculum: An Analysis and Interpretation* (Washington: Association of American Colleges, 1972), 62-67.

6 Watson Kirkconnell and A.S.P. Woodhouse, *The Humanities in Canada* (Ottawa: Humanities Research Council of Canada, 1947), 5.

7 See Keith R. Bridston and Dwight W. Culver, *Pre-Seminary Education* (Minneapolis: Augsburg, 1965), 55. See also J. Paul Williams, "But Don't Major in Religion!" *Christian Century*, 71, 24 (June 16, 1954): 731-32.

8 On this debate, see J. Allen Easley, "The Statement on Pre-Theological Studies," *Journal of Bible and Religion* (July 25, 1957); J. Arthur Baird, "Pre-Theological Training: An Empirical Study," *Journal of Bible and Religion* (October 27, 1959); and Ernest C. Colwell, "Integration of Pre-Seminary and Seminary Curricula," in *The Making of Ministers*, ed. Bridston and Culver, 116-30.

9 Note that *Crisis in the Humanities* (ed. J.H. Plumb [Baltimore: Penguin, 1964]) appeared in the same year that the Department of Religious Studies was established at UBC.

10 Welch, *Religion in the Undergraduate Curriculum*, 72, indicates that 72 percent of the public institutions with a program in Religious Studies offered one or more courses in Old Testament and New Testament.

11 Welch, *Religion in the Undergraduate Curriculum*, 72-73, indicates that only 36 percent of public institutions offered courses in a specific eastern religion. However, it was the public institutions that took the lead in developing the study of eastern religions in their programs of religious studies.

12 As one of the three western religions, there were many good reasons for including the Islamic tradition in the religious studies program at UBC, but it was somewhat unusual in the sense that, as Welch has pointed out, only 18 percent of the public institutions in his survey offered any courses in this tradition. See Welch, *Religion in the Undergraduate Curriculum*, 72.

13 For a list of courses dealing with religion and its cognate disciplines at UBC, see Appendix 1.

14 Robert N. Bellah, "Introduction," in *Religion and America*, ed. Douglas and Tipton, ix-xiii.

15 University of British Columbia, *Department of Religious Studies Undergraduate Courses, 1993-1994*, 6.

16 University of British Columbia, *Department of Religious Studies Undergraduate Courses 1993-1994*, 14.

17 The graduate faculty consists of Paul Mosca in Hebrew language and Bible, Paul Burns in patristics and Christian thought, Hanna Kassis in Islamic studies and sacred art and architecture, Richard Menkis in modern Jewish history and Judaism in Canada, and Dietmar Neufeld in Christian scriptures and the origins of Christianity. Graduate faculty from outside the department include Ashok Aklujkar in Sanskrit and Indian philosophy, Donald Baker in Korean religions and thought, Daniel Overmyer in Chinese religions and thought, and Harjot Oberoi in Sikh studies, all from the Department of Asian Studies. See University of British Columbia, *Department of Religious Studies Graduate Program*, 1-2.

18 Claude Welch, "Identity Crisis in the Study of Religion? A First Report from the ACLS Study," *Journal of the American Academy of Religion*, 39, 1 (March 1971): 6.

19 For a recent examination of the community colleges in Canada and their contribution to post-secondary education, see John D. Dennison and Paul Gallagher, *Canada's Community Colleges: A Critical Analysis* (Vancouver: University of British Columbia Press, 1986).

20 See George Marsden, "The Collapse of American Evangelical Academia," in *Faith and Rationality: Reason and Belief in God*, ed. Alvin Plantinga and Nicholas Wolterstoff (Notre Dame: University of Notre Dame Press, 1983), 219-64; Mark A. Noll, "The University Arrives in America, 1870-1930: Christian Traditionalism During the Academic Revolution," in *Making Higher Education Christian: The History and Mission of Evangelical Colleges in America*, ed. Joel A. Carpenter and Kenneth W. Shipps (Grand Rapids: Eerdmans, 1987), 98-109; and David Riesman, "The Evangelical Colleges: Untouched by the Academic Revolution," *Change*, 13, 1 (January-February, 1981): 13-20.

21 See Harold W. Boon, "The Development of the Bible College or Institute in the United States and Canada since 1880 and Its Relationship to the Field of Theological Education in America" (DEd thesis, New York University, 1950). See

also N. Keith Clifford, "The History of Protestant Theological Education in Canada," *Papers of the Canadian Society of Church History, 1989.*

22 David R. Elliott, "Knowing No Borders: Canadian Contributions to American Fundamentalism," in *Amazing Grace: Evangelicalism in Australia, Britain, Canada, and the United States,* ed. George A. Rawlyk and Mark A. Noll (Montreal and Kingston: McGill-Queen's University Press, 1994), 353-54.

23 See Ronald George Sawatsky, "Looking for that Blessed Hope: The Roots of Fundamentalism in Canada, 1878-1914" (PhD thesis, University of Toronto, 1985).

24 John McNicol, "Principal's Report," *Recorder,* 26 (June 1920): 4, cited in Stackhouse, *Canadian Evangelicalism,* 60.

25 Stackhouse, *Canadian Evangelicalism,* 63-66. Stackhouse characterizes Toronto Bible College as "transdenominational, Bible-centred, missions-oriented, spiritually vital, and fundamentally practical in its training." These characteristics it held in common with most other North American Bible colleges. At the same time, however, certain features set it apart. These were "its emphasis upon faculty who had strong academic qualifications, its concomitant appreciation for university education, its relations with a broad range of denominations, and its eschewing of dispensationalism." See Stackhouse, *Canadian Evangelicalism,* 70.

26 For an excellent discussion of the Bible-centred curriculum, see Virginia Lieson Brereton, "The Bible Schools and Conservative Evangelical Higher Education, 1880-1940," in *Making Higher Education Christian,* ed. Carpenter and Shipps, 110-36.

27 See Robert J. Hilgenberg, "English Bible," in *Toward a Harmony of Faith and Learning: Essays on Bible College Curriculum,* ed. Kenneth O. Gangel (Farmington Hills: William Tyndale College Press, 1983), 3-17.

28 See the Trinity Western University, *1993/94 Academic Calendar,* 11.

29 See the second page of the "Application for Admission" form contained at the back of the Trinity Western University *Calendar,* 12.

30 Kenneth R. Davis to Peter Remnant, 1 December 1981, *Dean of Arts Files,* UBC.

31 Peter Remnant to Kenneth R. Davis, 26 January 1982, *Dean of Arts Files,* UBC.

32 Robert M. Will to Daniel R. Birch, 10 October 1985, *Dean of Arts Files,* UBC.

33 Craig A. Evans to Kenneth Davis, 25 November 1981, *Dean of Arts Files,* UBC.

34 As Claude Welch noted in *Graduate Education in Religion: A Critical Appraisal* (Missoula: University of Montana Press, 1971), viii, "almost nothing has been written concerning graduate studies in religion, as distinct from theological education." Since all graduate degrees in religion are assumed to be professional degrees, none of the major surveys of graduate education in the United States have included graduate education in religion. The same is true in Canada. Robin S. Harris, in *A History of Higher Education in Canada 1663-1960* (Toronto: University of Toronto Press, 1976), deals with theology under professional education but he does not discuss graduate studies in the theological colleges. He notes the establishment of the Faculty of Divinity (since 1970, the Faculty of Religious Studies) at McGill in 1948 and the establishment of the

Toronto Graduate School of Theology in 1944, but he does not discuss graduate studies or degrees in these schools.

35 For a broader discussion of this problem, see Clifford, "History of Protestant Theological Education in Canada."

36 Robert Wood Lynn, "Notes Toward a History: Theological Encyclopedia and the Evolution of Protestant Seminary Curriculum, 1808-1968," *Theological Education*, 17, 2 (Spring 1981): 118-44.

37 On the question of curriculum, see Nora L. Hughes, "A History of the Development of Ministerial Education in Canada from Its Inception until 1925 in Those Churches Which Were Tributary to the United Church of Canada" (PhD thesis, Divinity School, University of Chicago, 1945), 52-55.

38 The best discussion of the origins and development of the four-fold program in theological education from Schleiermacher to the present is contained in Edward Farley, *Theologia: The Fragmentation and Unity of Theological Education* (Philadelphia: Fortress Press, 1983).

39 Samuel Blizzard was Professor of Christianity and Society at Princeton Theological Seminary. Throughout the 1950s, Blizzard gathered and analyzed data on the self-conception of Protestant clergy in the United States. The six "practitioner roles" he identified were preacher, teacher, priest, organizer, administrator, and pastor. His key articles are "The Minister's Dilemma," *Christian Century*, 73, 17 (25 April 1956): 508-10; "The Protestant Minister's Integrating Roles," *Religious Education*, 53, 4 (July-August 1958): 374-80; and "The Parish Minister's Self-Image of His Master Role," *Pastoral Psychology*, 9, 89 (December 1958): 25-32.

40 A thorough review of these studies and discussions between 1955 and 1985 is found in James Gustafson, assisted by Tod D. Swanson, "Reflections on the Literature on Theological Education Published between 1955 and 1985," *Theological Education Supplement II*, 24 (1988), 9-86.

41 Charles L. Taylor, "Report on the Development of an Ecumenical Theological Centre in Vancouver, BC" (unpublished report to the Joint Committee of the Boards of Anglican Theological College and Union College, 1969).

42 James P. Martin, *Exposure and Reflection: Toward First Principles* (Vancouver: Vancouver School of Theology, 1972).

43 The most thorough account of the founding principles and design of the VST competence curriculum is found in James P. Martin, "Competence Model Education," *Theological Education*, 13, 2 (Winter 1977): 125-36. The current understanding of the curriculum and the programs and degrees offered by the school are described in Vancouver School of Theology, *1993-1995 Calendar*, 24-36.

44 Key documents that describe some of the thinking leading to these changes are James P. Martin, "Vision for Mission," and Arthur Van Seters, "VST—Present Discernment and Future Vision," in *The Journey Continues: The Diamond Jubilee Lectures Celebrating Sixty Years of Theological Education, 1927-1987*, ed. R. Gerald Hobbs (Vancouver: Vancouver School of Theology, 1988), 70-85 and 46-69.

45 *Self-Study Report for The Association of Theological Schools in the United States and Canada* (Vancouver: Vancouver School of Theology, 1980), 47-48,

and *Self-Study Report for The Association of Theological Schools in the United States and Canada* (Vancouver: Vancouver School of Theology, 1992), 27-31.

46 For a fuller description of the development and character of this innovative program, see James N. Pankratz, "Globalization Begins at Home," *Theological Education*, 27, 2 (1991): 68-86. An example of the different approaches to the traditional disciplines being explored through the Native Ministries Degree Program is to be found in Brian J. Fraser, "Exploring New Approaches in the Native Ministries Degree Programme at Vancouver School of Theology," *Theological Education*, 29, 2 (Spring 1993): 73-89.

47 James M. Houston, "The History and Assumptions of Regent College," *Openness to the Future, a Prelude to Planning* (Vancouver: Regent College, 1974), 3-5. For the complete listing of current degrees and programs, see Regent College, *Catalogue 1993-1995*, 24-33.

48 *Report on Institutional Self-Study in Support of Application for Accreditation by the Association of Theological Schools*, vol. 1 (Vancouver: Regent College, 1984), 7.

49 In 1990, Regent entered into a cooperative agreement with these organizations for the training of staff people. See Regent College, *Catalogue 1993-1995*, 66.

50 Regent College, *Catalogue 1993-1995*, 31-32.

51 Associated Canadian Theological Schools, *1993/94 Calendar*, 9.

3

Faculty, Research, and Publications[*]

The institutions in British Columbia that now offer degree programs in the study of religion reached their present form in the 1960s and the 1970s. Because of their pioneering nature, the opportunities their faculties had to build up new traditions were unusual. But now, after a period of consolidation, similar opportunities to develop in new directions are presenting themselves. By the early 1980s, many in the generation of scholars who founded these institutions and programs had moved to other institutions or retired. The rest will retire by the mid-1990s. The late 1990s, then, will mark significant changes in the study of religion as a new generation begins to take over in a new context requiring a new agenda. This chapter will explore the nature and role of the founding generation of faculty members in the various institutions in establishing traditions of teaching, research, and publication. Further, it will explore the ways in which the institutional and programmatic isolation of the study of religion in BC between religious studies and theological studies and between differing approaches to theological studies were reinforced or mitigated by those activities.

The Department of Religious Studies at UBC

The decision to offer courses and programs in five of the living religions of the world had a determining influence on the makeup of the faculty in UBC's Department of Religious Studies. The sudden

---

[*] The notes to Chapter 3 are on pp. 103-104.

increase in enrolments in the late 1960s and the equally dramatic drop in the late 1970s, combined with the internal strife in the department throughout the 1970s, made planning for orderly growth in faculty resources difficult.

The department's faculty expansion was slow. William Nicholls was hired as professor of religious studies in 1961 and became head when the department was created in 1964, a position he held until he retired in 1983. Born in England in 1921, Nicholls studied classics and theology at St. John's College, Cambridge, graduating in 1949. He was travelling secretary for the World Student Christian Federation in Geneva from 1949 until 1951, spent an additional year of study at Wells Theological College, and served as an Anglican priest in England and Scotland from 1952 until 1960. He was appointed associate professor of systematic theology and church history at St. John's College, University of Manitoba in 1960 and moved to the University of British Columbia in 1961. In the 1950s, Nicholls published in the fields of ecumenism and worship. His interests in the 1960s, after coming to Canada, shifted to systematic and philosophical theology, and especially theological anthropology. He published *Systematic and Philosophical Theology*, volume I in the *Pelican Guide to Modern Theology* series, in 1969. Nicholls served on the founding committee of the Canadian Society for the Study of Religion from 1965-66 and its executive committee from 1968-71. He was the founding editor-in-chief of *Studies in Religion/Sciences Religieuses* from 1971-73 and served on its editorial board from 1973-83. By the 1970s, his interests in theological anthropology had come to focus on identity in religion and psychiatry. In 1972, he co-authored *I AMness: The Discovery of the Self Beyond the Ego*, with Vancouver therapist Ian Kent. After retirement, his work in religion and psychiatry continued and he developed new interests in Jewish-Christian relations.

As the department grew, it focused on four main areas, namely, Christian thought, Near Eastern studies, Buddhist and Hindu studies, and religious history. Nicholls's teaching and research was in the area of Christian thought. After his retirement, no appointment was made in this area until Paul Burns was given a tenure-track position in 1992. Burns was a Basilian priest and a patristic scholar who had served for many years as principal of St. Mark's College. The second area was Near Eastern studies and the second professor in religious studies at UBC was Charles Anderson, appointed to teach New Testament and Christian origins in 1962. Anderson was an American Methodist who completed a BD at Union Theological Seminary in New York, though he never became ordained; he proceeded to do graduate work at Columbia University. Hanna Kassis arrived in the summer of 1964 with a PhD from Harvard University in Near Eastern languages and literature; he was hired to teach Judaism and Hebrew scriptures. His research interests, and eventually his teaching, focused on Islam and Muslim-Christian relations. Larry Fine was the first appointment to the position in Judaic studies, teaching at UBC from 1974 until 1977. His doctorate in medieval Jewish mysticism was from Brandeis. He was followed in the Judaic position by Moshe Amon from 1977 to 1984. Amon did his doctorate in political philosophy at Claremont Graduate School and worked in the areas of terrorism, Judaism, and modernism. The position remained vacant until 1986 when Richard Menkis was appointed. Menkis did a BA and MA in medieval studies at the University of Toronto, then a MA and PhD at Brandeis in modern Judaic studies. Paul Mosca came in 1974 to teach Hebrew Bible and Near Eastern religions. His MA and PhD were from Harvard and his research interests included Phoenician language and culture and their later developments in Carthaginian language and culture. In the third area, Buddhist and Hindu studies, Arthur Link moved from the University of Michigan to UBC in 1964 to teach Buddhism. His doctoral work at Berkeley was in East Asian languages and he continued to translate the works of Buddhist monks in China until his death in 1975. Joseph I. Richardson came to the UBC faculty in 1967 after several years as dean of Carey Hall, first in the Department of Asian Studies and then in Religious Studies, to teach Indian religions. Richardson was a Baptist with a BD from McMaster University in Hamilton, Ontario. He taught in a Serampore Affiliated college in India and completed a STM at Union-Columbia while on a Rockefeller Fellowship in Advanced Religious Studies. In 1968, Shotaro Iida was appointed to the second position in Buddhism. His PhD was from the University of Wisconsin and his research interests were Indian and Tibetan Buddhism. Leon Hurvitz was jointly appointed by the Departments of Religious Studies and Asian Studies in 1971, where he remained until his retirement in 1989. The fourth area was religious history. Keith Clifford, a United Church minister whose doctoral work under Geoffrey Nuttal at the University of London dealt with Puritanism, came to the department in 1970 from the Divinity School at the University of Chicago, where he had been assistant dean of students. Previously, he had been minister at United Church at St. Augustine's United Church in Winnipeg and had served as General Secretary of the Student Christian Movement on the UBC campus.

The majority of the early faculty in the Department of Religious Studies at UBC were a "transitional generation," that is to say, a generation that was trained, for the most part, in Christian theological colleges and adapted the theological disciplines of bible, theology, and church history to the context of the secular university. The generation that will take over the department in the next decade will be trained differently. Most will be educated, in whole or in part, in departments of religious studies rather than in theological colleges. There will be an element of continuity because the majority of them will be trained by the transitional generation, but there will also be significant discontinuity because they will challenge and question the assumptions and methods of their predecessors. Furthermore, unless Canadian immigration and labour laws change in the meantime, the vast majority of this new generation will be Canadians by birth, though many will have received part of their graduate education elsewhere. Any analysis of the history and future of the Department of Religious Studies at UBC must keep this generation shift in faculty in mind. Equally important to keep in mind are the principles and policies of university departments of religious studies as they relate to the selection of teachers now that the discipline is well established and clearly defined.

While the establishment of departments of religious studies at Canadian universities took place during a period of university expansion, the transfer of power to the new generation of faculty will take place as university budgets are shrinking. New positions will be few and far between. There will be an increasing use of part-time lecturers and adjunct faculty drawn from other departments or colleges. Political skill and the will to survive in times of financial restraint will be essential for the continuation of the program in religious studies at UBC. The current signs are positive. Paul Mosca has been appointed head of the department. Paul Burns has been appointed to a tenure-track position. Dietmar Neufeld, with his doctorate in New Testament from McGill, has replaced Chuck Anderson in Christian origins, and a new position has been created in religion and culture to be filled in 1995. Enrolments of 788 in religious studies courses in 1992-93, with 40 students in the majors and honours programs, represent a significant reversal of the low numbers of the late 1970s and early 1980s. By 1994-95 the numbers had risen to over a thousand taking courses and over 60 enrolled in majors and honours programs. Most important of all, the university administration has recognized the importance of its program in religious studies and has taken steps to secure its place in the curriculum by consolidating the department with Classics while leaving the program with its own identity.

Vancouver School of Theology

Two goals lay at the heart of the original vision of theological education developed by the founders of the Vancouver School of Theology. First, they set out to create an ecumenical theological centre that would provide: (1) education for professional ministries in the sponsoring denominations, (2) facilities for the advanced study of theology and theological research, (3) lay education, (4) denominational formation, and (5) "an ecumenical forum for theological dialogue among persons of different disciplines and different theological viewpoints."[1] Second, they set out to design a curriculum that reflected their dissatisfaction with older, more formal systems of theological education and their conviction that there needed to be a close relationship between theological understanding and experience reflected in curricular design.[2] These goals were clearly identified in Charles Taylor's report in 1969, as was the need for a new faculty that would create a new image for the school. Taylor argued that the traditional disciplines of theological studies — Old Testament, New Testament, church history, theology and the philosophy of religion, ethics, liturgics, pastoral theology and counselling, missiology, homiletics, and Christian education — had to be represented in the new faculty, but these teachers should be willing to accept the aims and methods of the new program and focus their teaching on the development of competence in ministry and on the integration of the disciplines in the service of the church's mission.[3]

In the spring of 1972, the new Senate and Board of Governors of VST established very specific criteria for the selection of faculty. Teamwork and an ability to integrate the traditional disciplines in probing the issues raised by the task of training people for ministry were crucial. Dedicated church involvement was equally important. Other criteria mentioned were guidance by personal example, ecumenical commitment, teaching ability, parish experience, and a degree of enthusiasm that would stimulate and encourage others.[4] The Faculty Handbook, developed in 1977, listed the following as criteria for promotion: teaching ability; scholarly research and production, professional and creative work; service to the school and community; concern for the ministry; spiritual and moral contribution to the school community; interest in educational development; and promise of growing competence.[5] Together, the criteria for selection and promotion describe the kind of founding faculty sought by the school to implement its vision of a new kind of theological education.

Under the leadership of Principal James P. Martin, the vision of competence in ministry and integration of disciplines was further refined. In his inaugural address, Martin pointed to the identity and credibility of the church as the key issues facing the school in a time when the church's self-understanding was "becoming more and more dissipated into individualistic pietism on the one hand and worldly identification on the other."[6] For Martin, the identity of the church was formed by its Christology. The question of credibility could not be answered by adapting to present day change, but by adapting to Christ, crucified and risen and a forerunner of the new humanity, so that the church is "free to engage the present without falling victim to it."[7] Within the broader humanism of the university and contemporary society, the church is called to declare the incredibility of the Gospel:

> Finally, if the Church and its schools were asked to demonstrate Christian humanism to others who do not share its origin, they could only invite them to "repent and believe the gospel." But the Church will be credible in this invitation only when it confesses that it did not create the gospel but was created by it.[8]

Martin's views were heavily influenced by Karl Barth's theology of the word and Jürgen Moltmann's theology of the cross, and led VST to approach theological studies and education for ministry with its primary focus on the church and its mission in contemporary society.

Between 1972 and 1977, Martin, who became professor of New Testament as well as principal, assembled a faculty of eleven who shared this vision and were willing to be creative in implementing it. Of the 11, only one had received his doctorate from a university department of Near Eastern studies. Nine others received their doctorates from faculties of divinity or theological seminaries. Seven studied in the United States, two in Europe, and one in Canada. Only one had not completed his doctoral thesis. All had pastoral experience of some kind, though none for more than six years in the parish; two had only part-time pastoral experience while studying. None could be considered senior, well-established scholars in their fields or experienced pastors. The faculty was comprised young men in their thirties and forties in the early years of their careers who were willing to embark on an experiment in theological education.

Jim Martin, not surprisingly, was the oldest and most experienced. He was 49 when he came in 1972 and had taught at Princeton and Union, Richmond, for 13 years. His doctoral thesis at Princeton dealt with New Testament eschatology. Subsequent articles focused on Biblical interpretation and appeared in a wide range of journals and volumes representing a variety of theological viewpoints. While at Union, he had served as managing editor of *Interpretation: A Journal of Bible and Theology*, published under the auspices of the seminary.

Bill Crockett graduated from Trinity College in Toronto, did his doctorate at the Divinity School, University of Chicago, in patristics, and came to the Anglican Theological College in 1964 at the age of 30. He published on sacramental theology and drafted liturgies for the Anglican Liturgical Consultation in Canada. Terry Anderson did a BD at St. Stephen's, Edmonton, and a doctorate in Christian social ethics under Reinhold Niebuhr and John Bennett at Union Theological Seminary in New York. He taught at St. Stephen's College, Edmonton for three years and for another three at Union, Richmond, prior to moving to Vancouver at the age of 40 in 1973. His interests have been in bioethics, ethics and resource development, and the rights and claims of native peoples, and his publications have been mainly in church-related journals and volumes. Lloyd Gaston's doctorate in New Testament was from Basel in Switzerland; he taught for 10 years at Macalester College in Minnesota. He was 44 when appointed to VST in 1973. His early interest was in the Synoptics; his interest later shifted to Paul, and then to Jesus. A primary concern for Gaston was understanding and challenging the Christian roots of anti-Semitism. Jim Cruickshank graduated from Emmanuel College in Saskatoon and in 1970 completed a DRel at Chicago in religion and human development, with a focus on both personal and social transformation. He spent three years as a parish priest in the Diocese of the Cariboo from 1962-65 and was Director of the Sorrento Centre for Human Development, an Anglican lay training centre, for the next eight years prior to coming to VST as director of Field Education and associate professor of Pastoral Theology in 1973. Jim Lindenberger graduated with a BD and a ThM from Union, Richmond, and went on to do a doctorate at Johns Hopkins in Near Eastern studies, specializing in Aramaic language and literature. He was 33 when he came to VST, immediately after completing his doctorate in 1974. His research and publications explore Hebrew and Aramaic letters. Elly Bradley had a BD from Emmanuel College, Toronto and had completed the course work for a doctorate in religious education at Union Theological Seminary in New York. He served the Cartwright-Mather pastoral charge in Manitoba from 1962 until 1966. Between 1967 and 1974, he served as professor of Practical Theology and director of Continuing Education at the University of Winnipeg, where he developed a number of innovative programs in field education, continuing education, and lay leadership. In 1974, at the age of 41, he moved to VST as assistant professor of Educational Ministries and director of Continuing Education. Bill Adams did his BD at Bexley Hall and his MA and PhD at Princeton. He came to VST in 1975 at the age of 35, after graduate work and four years in parish ministry, as Anglican chaplain and assistant professor of Liturgics and Church History. Gerald Hobbs studied in Europe after completing a BD at Emmanuel College in Toronto. In his doctorate at Strasbourg, he examined Martin Bucer's commentary on the Psalms. Hobbs came to VST in 1977 at the age of 35, after three years as registrar and assistant professor of religious studies at Huntingdon College, Laurentian University, Sudbury, and three years at the Institut d'Histoire de la Reformation in Geneva. The history of Biblical interpretation, especially during the Reformation, remained the focus of his research and publication. Canadian holiness movements, church music, and hymnology were also areas of interest in which Hobbs researched and published. William J. (Bud) Phillips's doctoral studies at Boston University explored the use of the media in the continuing education of clergy; this remained a primary focus for his research and publication. After arriving at VST in 1977 at the age of 41, he developed new interests in the area of congregational studies. Previous training, including a BA from the University of

Alberta (Social Psychology) and a BD from McMaster University (Homiletics and Religious Education), prepared Phillips for a practical approach to the church and to the education of ministers, as reflected in his writing and teaching. As director of graduate studies and extension programs, Phillips applied his experience as a media communicator and trainer to the church at large. David Lochhead did all his post-secondary education at McGill University in Montreal. He was 42 when appointed to VST in 1978. His PhD thesis in the Philosophy of Religion was entitled "The Autonomy of Theology: A Critical Study with Special Reference to the Theology of Karl Barth and Contemporary Analytical Philosophy." His research and publications deal with theological method, Biblical interpretation, interfaith dialogue, and the interface between theology and modern technology. In addition to these faculty positions, in 1977 the school created the postition of teaching pastor, whose role it was to teach practice of ministry and advise students, with incumbency limited to three years at the school. The first appointment was Ralph Donnelly, a United Church minister from the Manitoba Conference, where he had served the Carroll Pastoral Charge from 1958 until 1965 and Immanuel United Church and one of its predecessors in Winnipeg from 1965 until 1977.

One striking commonality in the founding generation of faculty at VST was the connection with Union Theological Seminary in Richmond, Virginia, a pioneering institution in the development of a competence model for theological education. Martin taught there for ten years prior to coming to Vancouver; Anderson had taught at Union for four years. Lindenberger did his BD and ThM at Richmond. Another important element in the founding faculty's experience was their creative efforts to serve their respective churches in continuing and lay education. Bradley came from the University of Winnipeg, where he had developed an extensive program of pastors' groups and lay education events in which faculty from the college travelled to various locales across the province. Cruickshank had served as director of an Anglican lay education centre for eight years. Phillips's work at McMaster included the development of self-directed study programs, the production of media resources for distance education, and the offering of degree programs in evening courses and summer schools. In addition, he had his own consulting firm that arranged seminars for business, education, church bodies, and government in the field of leadership training.

Surprisingly, few of the founding faculty had extensive pastoral experience in congregations or parishes. Although all had served in some capacity as student assistants or summer supply, only Lochhead and Phillips had five years or more as the sole clergy after ordination. All but Crockett and Cruickshank were new to the sponsoring churches in British Columbia. Martin and Lindenberger joined the United Church of Canada and Adams the Anglican Church of Canada. Gaston remained an American Presbyterian, with his lines lodged in the Presbytery of North Puget Sound, while Phillips continued as a Baptist.

A considerable amount of time and energy went into the design and implementation of the new competence curriculum during VST's first decade. Nevertheless, the faculty researched and published in their respective disciplines, mostly in the popular and academic journals of their denominations and theological disciplines. Several served as officers in their respective learned societies and served on editorial committees for church and learned journals. Most served on church committees at the local, regional, and national levels and contributed papers and reports in their areas of expertise. All were active in the continuing and lay education work of VST.

In preparation for the self-study and accreditation visit of the Association of Theological Schools in 1980, the founding faculty, together with others connected with the school, reviewed the decade of developments at the Vancouver School of Theology. As principal, Jim Martin again drew much of this study and discussion together in his address at the beginning of the fall term. It took the form of an exegesis of the school's new statement of purpose, which read:

> The purpose of Vancouver School of Theology is to provide education that will enable men and women to become pastor / theologians and lay / theologians in the ministries of the churches in changing social contexts. In response to God's redemptive activity, the School seeks to be faithful to the Lordship of Christ in the mission of the church in the whole of creation.[9]

He pointed out that a major shift in emphasis had taken place for the school in the adoption of the statement. The organizing principle, or "defensible centre," of the curriculum had moved from "professional education for ministry" to "the mission of the church."[10] It was mission that defined ministry, not the other way around.

Martin's involvement on the United Church of Canada's Task Force on Theological Education for the 1980s was a major stimulus for this change.[11]

This shift in vision played a significant role in the selection of Martin's successor as principal in 1983. Arthur Van Seters had spent a month of his sabbatical leave in 1981 in Costa Rica and Nicaragua, working on liberation theology and the social dimensions of biblical interpretation and preaching. The shift in focus within the school from individual professional learning to the social purpose of the learning coincided with shifts in Van Seters' own approach to theological studies and education.[12] Since 1973, he had been executive director of the Montreal Institute for Ministry (affiliated with McGill University), a creation of the Anglican, United, and Presbyterian theological colleges in Montreal, that provides a final year of practical and ecclesiastical education in their MDiv programs. In addition, he was an instructor in Old Testament in the Faculty of Religious Studies at McGill from 1976 until 1983. He was familiar with competence education for ministry, having spent four years at Union, Richmond, doing his doctorate in Old Testament.

Though the core of the founding faculty remained in place, several changes in and additions to the faculty took place in the 1980s. In 1980, the position of teaching pastor went to Morar Murray-Hayes, a graduate of McGill and a United Church minister in Richmond Hill, Ontario. She became the first woman teaching full-time at the school, though not in a tenure-track position. Jim Cruickshank left in 1982 to become dean of the Cathedral in Vancouver and was replaced as director of field education and assistant professor of ministry by another Canadian Anglican, Jim McCullum. McCullum was a native of BC and a graduate of Wycliffe College in Toronto. From 1963 until 1982, he held pastorates in Dawson City, Whitehorse, Trail, Kelowna, and Vancouver; he had spent a sabbatical year at William Temple College in Rugby, England, working with industrial missions. His DMin was begun after his appointment to VST and his thesis examined the use of narrative theology in a mission-based curriculum. Murray-Hayes completed her three-year appointment in 1983 and was not replaced. Instead, the school created a tenure-track position in pastoral theology and appointed Mary Weir, a United Church minister who had completed a doctorate in the feminist theology of Rosemary Reuther from St. Mary's College at St. Andrew's University in Scotland in 1983. Weir had served as a missionary of the Presbyterian Church in the United States in Zaire from 1969 until 1974, teaching at the Protestant Faculty of Theology at the National University. She was profoundly deaf, and focused her research and writing on the role of women and the disabled in the church. Brian Fraser was added to the faculty when the Presbyterian Church in Canada and St. Andrew's Hall entered into an agreement of association and affiliation with VST in 1985. Fraser was a graduate of Knox College in Toronto, had worked on the social gospel among Canadian Presbyterians for his doctorate in Canadian history at York University, Toronto, and was minister at Glebe Presbyterian Church in Toronto for seven years. Subsequent research and publication concerned the history of ordained ministry and theological education in Canada. He sits on the Editorial Advisory Board of the *Toronto Journal of Theology*. Bill Adams left to teach in Texas in 1984 and was replaced by David Holton, a Vancouver-born Anglican liturgist and church historian who studied at Nashotah House Theological Seminary and the Institut Catholique in Paris. His research interests and publications followed from his doctoral work on the history of Czech liturgy. Holton, together with Bill Crockett, were key figures in the production of the *Book of Alternative Services* for the Anglican Church of Canada. Holton moved to Trinity College, Toronto, in 1987 and his position was filled by Richard Leggett, another Nashotah House graduate who was completing a doctoral thesis on the history of ordination rites in the Anglican tradition at Notre Dame University. Leggett had extensive experience in lay education during his six years as a priest in the Episcopalian Church in the United States and is currently vice-chair of the Doctrine and Worship Committee of the Anglican Church of Canada. Greer Anne Ng replaced Elly Bradley in Educational Ministries and as director of Lay Education when the latter resigned in 1986. Ng had taught at Trinity Theological College in Singapore, had completed a doctorate in English Literature at Columbia University in New York, and had extensive cross-cultural experience, especially with Pacific Rim churches. She had spent the five years prior to coming to VST as Christian Development Officer with the Hamilton Conference of the United Church of Canada and had written curriculum and devotional materials for the church. Her research and publications reflect an interest in cross-cultural education and globalization in theological education. She serves on the editorial board of *Religious Education*, the journal of the Religious Education Association of the United States and Canada. Mary Weir left to become a chaplain at Northwestern University in Chicago in 1988 and was replaced by Janet Cawley, another United Church minister with a doctorate from Toronto and experience as an intentional interim-minister. Her doctoral thesis dealt with the power dynamics underlying the negotiations for union between the Anglican and United Churches of Canada between the 1940s and the 1970s; her research and publications focused on feminist theology from a Jungian perspective. Cawley resigned in 1992 to return to the parish. Nancy Cocks, a Presbyterian minister with a ThD in Calvin and hermeneutics from Knox College, Toronto School of Theology, who had spent three years as associate secretary for Faith and Witness at the Canadian Council of Churches, was hired for the revived position of teaching pastor at the school and teaches most of the courses that Cawley taught. The position is again a three-year term appointment rather than tenure-track. In 1993, Van Seters left to become principal of Knox College, Toronto, and was replaced by W.J. (Bud) Phillips. In 1994, Cocks was appointed to a tenure-track position in pastoral theology and has begun writing in the area of pastoral hermeneutics. Canadian Lutheran Harry Maier was appointed to replace the retiring Lloyd Gaston in New Testament. Maier was born and raised in Alberta, graduated from the Lutheran seminary in Saskatoon, and completed his doctoral work at Oxford in Christian origins. His research interests continue in that area and he takes a cultural-anthropological approach to the subject.

The second generation of faculty at VST reflected the shift in emphasis at the beginning of the 1980s. They were in their thirties and forties when appointed. The focus of their research was the practice of ministry in the mission of the church. They were active in the learned societies related to their disciplines and some held office in them. They sat on and were consulted regularly by regional and national church committees. They published in popular and academic journals related to their denominations and theological disciplines and in papers and reports for church committees. Unlike the first generation, most of them had their first full-time teaching appointment at VST. With the exception of Van Seters, none had studied or taught in a competence curriculum before coming to VST.

Regent College

The founders of Regent College, all of whom came from a Plymouth Brethren background, sought to create a graduate school of theological studies to provide Christians with an evangelical, biblical, and theological perspective on their lives in the world, whatever their vocation. The statement of faith of the World Evangelical Fellowship was adopted by the college, and subscription to it was required by all members of the Board, Senate, and teaching staff. The original intention was not to provide professional education, though those exploring some form of call to church service in North America or abroad were encouraged to take the programs. In the discussions concerning the establishment of the college, founding principal James Houston wrote, the focus shifted "from the committed Christian who wants to serve, to the questioning Christian who wants to know."[13] The first Board of the college included Brethren, Mennonites, Pentecostals, Baptists, and Presbyterians, reflecting the transdenominational character the founders sought to foster. Though individuals from these denominations were appointed by the Regent Board, they did not officially represent the denominations.

The founding faculty appointed in the early 1970s was small, and many of them worked part-time at the college. They represented two distinct generations of evangelical scholars from two different national traditions of evangelicalism. The older generation was British, while the younger generation was American. Both groups, however, represented what historians of American religion have called "the new evangelicalism," a reawakening within evangelical circles to the value of scholarship and research and engagement in public affairs. At the centre of this movement in the United States was Fuller Theological Seminary, founded in 1947, and *Christianity Today*, a biweekly magazine established in 1956.[14] In *Reforming Fundamentalism: Fuller Seminary and the New Evangelicalism*, George Marsden summarized the characteristics of the movement's leaders:

> They were intellectuals with immense confidence in the powers of argument. In their emphasis on intellect and higher education they were drawing particularly on the Calvinist legacy in their heritage. They were rejecting the types of revivalism and dispensationalism that were so culturally pessimistic and so preoccupied with saving souls that they had virtually withdrawn from the Western cultural

and intellectual heritage. The reformers were turning away in particular from the chief institutional sign of that withdrawal, the Bible institute. They were not interested in narrow Bible training. Rather, they were determined to produce a body of Christian writing that by force of argument would gain an audience even in the greatest intellectual centres of the civilization.[15]

At the same time, in Great Britain the Inter-Varsity Fellowship was playing a similar role in broadening the evangelical movement beyond its conservative base and evangelical scholars were establishing centres and forming organizations, such as Tyndale House at Cambridge and the Tyndale Fellowship for Biblical Research, both founded in 1945, to strengthen mutual support and influence in intellectual circles.[16] The American and British movements were different in constituency and ethos, but worked closely together in scholarly endeavours such as biblical commentaries, theological encyclopedias, and dictionaries of the Christian faith.[17]

Principal James Houston was a Scot, born in Edinburgh in 1922 and educated at Edinburgh and Oxford. He was a university lecturer in geography at Oxford and a fellow of Hertford College. After his arrival at Regent in 1969, he continued to teach geography at UBC and developed his interests in spirituality and prayer through his teaching at Regent. William J. Martin, formerly professor and head of the Department of Semitic Languages at the University of Liverpool and a prominent Brethren scholar, became vice principal (academic) and professor of Old Testament. While at Regent, he taught Hebrew in UBC's Department of Religious Studies and served on the team that produced the New International Version of the bible. Stanley M. Block, formerly chair of the Department of Industrial Engineering at the Illinois Institute of Technology, became vice principal (administration) in 1970, but remained only one year.

Carl Armerding and Ward Gasque, two young evangelical biblical scholars (35 and 30 years old respectively), were the first full-time professorial appointments. Though of Brethren background, both had done BD degrees, Armerding at Trinity Evangelical in Illinois and Gasque at Fuller in California. Armerding went on to Brandeis University to do a doctorate in Old Testament and Gasque to Manchester to do doctoral work in New Testament with F.F. Bruce. Armerding compared the heroic ages in Israel and Greece using literary-historical tools in his thesis, while Gasque examined the history of criticism related to the Acts of the Apostles. Armerding's subsequent research and writing focused on the prophets, biblical criticism from an evangelical perspective, and liberation theology and evangelicals. Gasque wrote on the Acts of Apostles and early Christian missions. Both belonged to the Evangelical Theological Society and the Tyndale Fellowship for Biblical Research and served at various times on the editorial board of *Christianity Today*. In addition, they were active participants in the meetings of the Society of Biblical Literature and the Canadian Society of Biblical Literature. Both edited and wrote for several dictionaries, encyclopedias, and biblical commentaries issued by evangelical publishers in Great Britain and the United States. Samuel Mikolaski, formerly principal of the Baptist Leadership Training School in Calgary, whose doctoral thesis at Oxford examined the objective doctrine of the Atonement in R.W. Dale, James Denney, and P.T. Forsyth, lectured part-time in systematic theology. Ian Rennie, minister at Fairview Presbyterian Church in Vancouver with a doctorate from Toronto in Puritanism, lectured in church history. In 1972, Rennie was appointed full-time in church history, and in 1974 Clark Pinnock was appointed as the first full-time professor in systematic theology. Pinnock did his doctorate in New Testament at the University of Manchester under F.F. Bruce and taught at Trinity Evangelical Divinity School prior to coming to Regent. Pinnock's reputation as one of the rising young scholars in North American evangelicalism was growing, and he attracted a significant number of new students to Regent. In the years immediately following his arrival, enrolments increased by 50 students a year. Larry Hurtado, with his MA from Trinity Evangelical and his PhD from Case Western, was appointed in New Testament in 1974.

In 1976, Bruce Waltke was appointed at the age of 46 to teach Old Testament. Waltke had studied at Dallas Theological Seminary, had doctorates in Old Testament from both Dallas and Harvard, and then returned to Dallas to teach for 18 years. He was a textual scholar and belonged to the Evangelical Theological Society and the Society of Biblical Literature. In 1985, he went to Westminster Seminary, but returned to teach at Regent in 1991. Klaus Bockmuehl came to Regent in 1977 at the age of 46 from St. Chrischona Bible Seminary in Germany. He had studied in England and at Basel, working as a research assistant for Jürgen Moltmann during his doctoral studies on the criticism of religion in Marx and Feurbach. He taught theology and ethics and wrote primarily in German on this topic. He was on the editorial board of the German equivalent to *Christianity Today*. Irving R. Hexham became assistant professor of the philosophy of religion in 1977. His doctorate in history and religious studies was from the University of Bristol. He had spent time as a lecturer at Bishop Lonsdale College in Derby and in the mission field in Africa, where his interest in Afrikaner and African religions grew. John L. Nolland was appointed assistant professor of New Testament in 1978. An Australian Anglican priest born in 1947, and a graduate of Moore Theological College with a doctorate from Cambridge, he published in the area of Christianity's encounter with other cultures during the New Testament period. The final appointment during the 1970s was James I. Packer, a well-known evangelical Anglican scholar from England who was 53 when he moved to Vancouver in 1979. In England, he had completed doctoral work on Richard Baxter with Geoffrey Nuttall at Oxford, served as director of Latimer House, a research centre at Oxford, and taught at Tyndale Hall, Bristol, and Trinity College, Bristol. He was visiting professor in several evangelical schools in North America and a member of the Evangelical Theological Society and the Tyndale Fellowship. Packer took the position in historical theology and wrote extensively on evangelical biblical interpretation and the knowledge of God.

The first generation of faculty at Regent was devoted to the graduate lay school of theology envisioned by its founders. The clear emphasis in the appointments was on biblical studies and interpretation. The majority of the faculty were part of the extensive networks of Anglo-American evangelicalism that developed following the Second World War. Several came from English Brethren and Anglican evangelicalism, especially the Tyndale Fellowship for Biblical Research. The North American networks of neo-evangelicalism, especially the Evangelical Theological Society and *Christianity Today*, were well represented. Many had some experience in pastoral ministry, but often as assistants while doing their graduate work. The focus of their interests was clearly academic rather than professional. The transfer of the principalship from Houston, who stayed on faculty as chancellor and professor of Spiritual Theology, to Carl Armerding in 1978 marked the beginning of a new era in the history of Regent that saw greater attention being paid to the education of professional church workers.

In 1979, Regent responded to growing pressure from its constituencies, especially the Baptist Union of Western Canada, and developed its MDiv program for those seeking ordination in their respective denominations. Carey Hall, the Baptist Union college on the UBC campus, first developed a one-year pastoral certificate to supplement the academic courses in Regent's MCS degree, then cooperated in the development of the full MDiv degree. Carey agreed to provide two-and-one-half faculty positions and put its resources into a joint library with Regent. Roy Bell was appointed principal and professor of pastoral studies at Carey Hall in 1980. Bell had chaired the Regent Board of Governors in 1972-73 while senior minister at First Baptist Church, Vancouver. Philip Collins moved from being the British Columbia area minister for the Baptist Union of Western Canada to the position of associate professor of applied theology and director of field education in 1980. His MDiv was from Gordon-Conwell Theological Seminary and his DMin from Fuller, with its focus on church growth. Collins became principal in 1984, when Bell accepted the call to be senior minister at First Baptist Church in Calgary. In 1988, Bell returned to Carey and Regent as Erb/Gullison Professor of Family Ministries. Guenter Strothotte, a Lutheran minister with a ThD from Erlangen University in Germany, moved from VST to become librarian for the new joint venture in 1981. In 1983, Samuel Mikolaski returned to Vancouver as Pioneer Macdonald Professor of Baptist Studies. He was principal of the Baptist Leadership Training School in Calgary in the early 1970s, taught at North American Baptist Seminary in Sioux Falls in the late 1970s, and served two years as president of the Atlantic Baptist College in Moncton, NB. In 1990, Mikolaski retired and was replaced by Stanley J. Grenz, who had been teaching at North American Baptist Seminary. Grenz had done his doctoral studies in Munich on the American Baptist leader, Isaac Backus. Subsequently, his focus shifted to the nature and role of evangelical theology and ethics in the late twentieth century, with a special interest in the theology of Wolfhart Pannenberg. John Zimmerman, an American Presbyterian with an MDiv from Princeton and a DMin from San Francisco Theological Seminary, became Charles Bentall Professor of Pastoral Studies in 1986.

New faculty with established names in evangelical circles, new facilities, the new MDiv program, and an aggressive strategy of public relations and recruitment that communicated the sense of adventure and innovation that marked the first decade of Regent's development — all served to increase student numbers significantly and made more appointments to the faculty possible. Faculty were encouraged to travel and lecture widely and the college kept its constituencies well-informed through *The Regent College Bulletin* and *Crux: A Quarterly Journal of Christian Thought and Opinion.* The latter began as an occasional journal of the Graduate Fellowship of Ontario. In 1979, Regent was asked to continue and expand the publication, with the faculty serving as the editorial board. It continues to be a primary vehicle for the expression of faculty views on the four major issues identified by James Houston in his inaugural editorial: emphasizing the centrality of biblical authority for the whole life of humanity before God and the world; renewing devotion in "a disciplined spirit of godly piety"; assuring Christians of faith and hope in thinking reflectively and acting responsibly as citizens in the world; and meeting the challenges of communicating Christian truth in the face of modern concepts of knowledge and disciplines of the mind.[18] The new appointments in the 1980s brought a combination of scholars with established reputations in evangelical circles, many of whom had been visiting lecturers at Regent, and younger scholars, several of whom had studied previously at Regent. In 1980, Sven Soderlund became the first Regent graduate to return to teach on the faculty. An ordained minister in the Pentecostal Assemblies of Canada, he completed a doctorate in Old Testament at Glasgow in 1978, focusing on the Septuagint version of Jeremiah, and lectured at Regent and UBC's Department of Religious Studies before being appointed full-time as assistant professor of biblical studies. Loren Wilkinson and Don Lewis were appointed in 1981, the former in interdisciplinary studies and philosophy to replace Hexham, who had moved to the Department of Religious Studies at the University of Manitoba, and the latter in church history to replace Ian Rennie, who had moved to the Ontario Theological Seminary. Wilkinson had a BA from Wheaton, an MA from Trinity Evangelical Divinity School, and a doctorate in the humanities from Syracuse University. Prior to coming to Regent, he taught English at Seattle Pacific University. His interests focused on ecology and the arts. Lewis was another graduate of Regent who did his doctorate in nineteenth-century English evangelicalism under P.B. Hinchliff at Balliol College, Oxford. Another biblical scholar, William Dumbrell, was appointed in 1984. Dumbrell was an Australian Anglican priest who served as vice president of Moore Theological College before coming to Regent. His BD and MTh were from the University of London and his doctorate in Old Testament from Harvard. His focus in research and writing was the covenant literature of the Old Testament and its unitary character. Gordon Fee, a prominent and widely published evangelical New Testament scholar with degrees from Seattle Pacific and Southern California, moved to Regent from Gordon-Conwell Theological Seminary in 1986. Previously he had taught at Wheaton College. Paul Stevens came to Regent in 1986 to teach applied theology after serving as teaching pastor at University Chapel in Vancouver. His BD was from McMaster and he earned his DMin from Fuller. The focus of his research and writing was Christian family life and equipping the ministry of the laity. Elmer Dyck also arrived in 1986 to teach biblical studies. He was a graduate of Winnipeg Bible College, Trinity Evangelical Divinity School, and McGill University. His PhD from the latter institution was in the canonical interpretation of Jonah and his research continues in canonical interpretation. Michael Green, an English Anglican whose writings on the New Testament and work in evangelism had given him a worldwide reputation in evangelical circles, came in 1987 as professor of evangelism, a position he held until returning to England in 1992. Walter C. Wright replaced Armerding as principal in 1988, assuming the position of professor of leadership and management, as well. Wright had a doctorate from Fuller Seminary and had worked and taught there before coming to Vancouver. Craig M. Gay became assistant professor of interdisciplinary studies in 1991, following the completion of a doctorate in the sociology of religion under Peter Berger at Boston University, with James Davison Hunter as the outside reader. David Diewart, another Regent graduate, returned to the college as assistant professor of biblical languages in 1991 after completing a PhD at the University of Toronto in the composition of the Elihu speeches. His research and writing explored Hebrew poetry and narratives. Thena Ayres, a former Inter-Varsity staff person, became assistant professor of adult education and director of extension in 1992. She was a graduate of UBC and completed an MA at Covenant Theological Seminary. She did her MEd and EdD at the University of Toronto in intercultural higher education. Eugene H. Peterson, an American Presbyterian whose writings on spirituality were widely known, was appointed as James M. Houston Professor of Spiritual Theology in 1993.

Regent inaugurated a Chinese Studies Program in 1985 to serve the growing needs of the Chinese church, both in Canada and abroad. The goal of the program was "to contribute to the understanding and renewal of Chinese culture in the light of Scripture." The first full-time faculty member and academic director of the Chinese studies program was Thomas In-sing Leung, a scholar whose interests focus on Chinese philosophy and culture. He was born and received his early education in Hong Kong and has a doctorate in philosophy from the University of Hawaii. In 1989, Edwin Hui was appointed as assistant professor of spiritual theology and medical ethics and program director of the Chinese studies program. He is a Regent graduate with an MD and PhD from UBC.

In sociologist James Davison Hunter's analysis of the impact of neo-evangelicalism on Christian orthodoxy in North America in the twentieth century, *Evangelicalism: The Coming Generation*, he suggested that the movement accepted a "code of political civility" that led to toleration of others' beliefs, opinions, and lifestyles and to an effort to be tolerable to others. The results were a weakening of the traditional symbolic boundaries of evangelicalism.

> A deep, compulsive, organic faith in the eternal and transcendent verities that emerge out of a quiet, taken-for-granted certainty is disappearing. It is not as though these Evangelicals no longer believe in God, his authority, or the authority of Scriptures, or the divine sanction of the traditions. It is that they have difficulty believing in these things simply and literally, the way a person would say that his neighbour exists. Once the belief that the central facts (carried by the traditions and taught by the churches) are facts in the most literal and absolute sense is weakened, traditional religion begins to disintegrate.... When these lose a sense of divine origin or divine sanction, or when they are seen as having a human and temporal origin, the believer's conviction is enfeebled.[19]

Regent faculty member Craig Gay reviewed Hunter's book for *Crux*[20] and later wrote the lead article in a faculty symposium on "The Uneasy Intellect of Modern Evangelicalism." At mid-century, he argued, the problem for evangelicals was separatism and abdication of intellectual responsibility. In the 1990s, the problem had shifted to "the hankering after 'relevance' and cultural recognition."[21] Regent's mission statement stated its determination to resist the drift that Hunter identified in the broader evangelical community as the 1990s began. "Recognizing that God calls his people," it read, "to claim the whole of human life for Jesus Christ as they spread the good news of his saving grace, the College shapes its corporate life to produce believers who can fulfil this calling with insight and skill in varied vocations world-wide."[22] Regent promised its supporters that it would "provide resources for developing a firm biblical faith,, nourished by the Christian heritage and marked by realism, thoughtfulness, intelligence, and integrity."[23] The faculty were convinced that they could hold evangelical conviction and intellectual integrity in creative tension.

The faculty selected by Regent College exemplified the determination of neo-evangelicalism to establish a credible intellectual presence in the midst of the university and to engage in dialogue with the leading disciplines and voices of the modern era. Their initial degrees were from evangelical schools, but their doctoral degrees were from the leading universities in their chosen fields.[24] Slightly more did their graduate work in England than in the United States, but all played an active role in North American evangelical organizations and networks beyond the college, as well as in the learned societies for their particular disciplines. The ways in which individual faculty members at Regent deal with this current ferment within evangelicalism vary,[25] but the institution itself represents that wing of evangelicalism that seeks a serious and honest engagement with modern culture.

Trinity Western University

Trinity Western University evolved from a bible college with 17 students in 1962 to a university with 1,558 students in 1993 and full membership and accreditation with the Association of Universities and Colleges of Canada. Throughout, Trinity Western has kept close ties with its sponsoring body, the Evangelical Free Church, a denomination of some 100,000 members in the United States and Canada that grew out of the Scandinavian free church movement in the 1880s. It operates Trinity Evangelical Divinity School and Trinity College in Deerfield, Illinois, as well as Trinity Western.

Most of the degree programs offered contain a requisite core of theological studies. Twelve semester hours in the Department of Religious Studies, including introductions to the Old and New Testament and a biblical content course, are required for the BA, BSc, and BEd degrees. The department offers courses in "theological studies" rather than "religious studies," as the terms are being used in this review. Twenty-four of the 54 courses offered in the department deal with the Bible, while only one deals with world religions. The reason is clearly stated in the introduction to the department's offerings in the Trinity Western calendar:

> The mission of the Department of Religious Studies is to produce graduates with an intelligent and lively understanding of the Bible as the inspired, inerrant, and authoritative Word of God and to develop a biblical yet critical discernment of what is truthful, good, and wholesome.... Biblical study should never be approached purely objectively. God is to be encountered, not just discussed, and the Scriptures obeyed, not just read. As you grow in your ability to apply scholarly tools to the biblical text, faculty will encourage you to ask, "How does the passage I'm studying apply to my own life?" Your maturing biblical comprehension will contribute to a deeper Christian understanding of your studies.[26]

Five of the seven full-time faculty in the department did their doctoral work in biblical studies. The other two are historians.

As in the case of Regent College, the growing number of programs and students at Trinity Western made growth in faculty numbers possible. Though the statement of faith to which faculty are required to subscribe "without reservation" is more detailed than that of Regent, and clearly premillennialist in stance,[27] Trinity Western adopted a similar strategy of appointing new faculty to its Division of Religious Studies from "the coming generation" of evangelicals with first degrees from evangelical schools and doctoral degrees from secular universities.

The first generation of faculty in the division, appointed in the mid-1970s and serving until the early 1980s, were largely without doctorates while they were teaching at Trinity Western. The exception was the first full-time professor in Religious Studies, Enoch E. Mattson, a graduate of Wheaton College with a ThD from Dallas Theological Seminary. Of the four colleagues who joined him in the early years of growth, A. Frederick Thompson had a BD from Episcopal Theological Seminary and Elmer Dyck, Raymond Bystrom, and Stanley Riegel were doctoral candidates at McGill, Manchester, and Aberdeen respectively. Bystrom and Riegel did not finish their degrees, while Dyck completed his and moved to Regent College as assistant professor of biblical studies in 1985.

In 1981, Craig A. Evans was appointed chair of the division, head of biblical studies, and professor of religious studies. He had a

MDiv from Western Baptist Seminary and completed his doctorate on the early Jewish and Christian interpretations of Isaiah 6:9-10 at Claremont Graduate School in 1983 under W.H. Brownlee. His research and publications dealt with the historical Jesus, the Gospels, the function of the Old Testament in the New, and the cultural context of the early Christian writings. In these, he worked closely with James A. Sanders at Claremont and James H. Charlesworth at Princeton. Craig C. Broyles came in 1985. He received a BA from Central Bible College in Missouri, a MSC from Regent College, and a PhD from the University of Sheffield on the psalms of lament under David J.A. Clines. A broad range of Old Testament studies and the principles of biblical interpretation formed the focus of his research and writing. James M. Scott arrived in 1990 as an assistant professor of biblical studies. His ThM was from Dallas Theological Seminary and his DTh from Tübingen. He worked with Peter Stuhlmacher on the theme of adoption in the Pauline corpus. Thomas F. Bulick was appointed in 1991. He did a ThM at Dallas Theological Seminary and is currently a doctoral candidate at the same institution. In 1992, Stanley E. Porter joined the division as an associate professor of religious studies. He had an MA from Trinity Evangelical Divinity School and a PhD in New Testament linguistics from the University of Sheffield. All four biblical scholars are active members of the Society of Biblical Literature. Further, all are engaged in editing and writing for major evangelical publishing houses, such as Eerdmans, Baker, Zondervan, and Inter-Varsity, and for the leading journals of biblical studies. Broyles and Porter are members of the Tyndale Fellowship of Biblical and Theological Research. All four have lectured widely in the network of evangelical colleges and societies in North America.

Kenneth R. Davis spent 10 years in pastoral ministries and teaching positions in the Baptist Convention of Ontario before beginning to teach in the history department at the University of Waterloo in 1967. He had received a MA in biblical literature from Wheaton in 1955 and completed his doctorate in history at the University of Michigan in 1971, exploring the intellectual origins of evangelical Anabaptism in the medieval ascetic tradition. He was appointed professor of history and religious studies at Trinity Western in 1980, as professor of church history at Trinity Western Seminary and coordinator of the Associated Canadian Theological Schools in 1988, and as dean of graduate affairs at Trinity Western in 1989. His research is focused on Anabaptism, education, and charismatic movements in Europe and North America. Douglas Shantz has a BA from Wheaton and an MA from Westminster Theological Seminary. His doctorate is in history from the University of Waterloo and his research interests are in the radical wing of the Reformation and the subsequent development of pietism. He was appointed assistant professor of religious studies in 1986.

Evans, Broyles, and Shantz all serve as adjunct faculty for the Associated Canadian Theological Schools at Trinity Western, with Davis acting as the consortium coordinator. The consortium consists of Canadian Baptist Seminary, sponsored by the Baptist General Conference of Canada, Northwest Baptist Theological Seminary, serving the Fellowship of Evangelical Baptist Church in Canada, and Trinity Western Seminary, established by the Evangelical Free Church of Canada. The disciplines represented by most of the regular faculty at ACTS are biblical foundations and practical application for ministry. Larry Perkins moved to Northwest from Toronto Baptist Seminary in 1978 to teach biblical studies. At that time, he had a BA in theology from Mansfield College in Oxford, an MA in Near Eastern studies from the University of Toronto, and had completed the course work for his doctorate from Toronto in Septuagintal studies under John Wevers. He became academic dean at Northwest in 1980 and was promoted to full professor in 1986. He serves on the Canadian Commission of the American Association of Bible Colleges and is a member of their Commission on Professional Development and Testing. His research interests include Markan and Petrine theology, septuagint studies, and demonology as it relates to Christology. Vern Steiner came to Trinity Western Seminary in 1990 as assistant professor of biblical studies. His MDiv and ThM were from Western Conservative Baptist Seminary and he received his PhD from Trinity Evangelical Divinity School in 1992. His thesis dealt with intertextuality and exegesis in the Asa narrative. His ongoing interests are in compositional analysis and exegetical method, especially in the narratives of the Old Testament. Donald Launstein taught systematics part-time at Northwest and ACTS while senior pastor at Maple Ridge Baptist from 1987 until 1992. Prior to this he had been professor of biblical literature and registrar at Western Conservative Baptist Seminary in Portland and president of Southwestern Conservative Baptist Bible College in Phoenix. He came to ACTS through Northwest as director of the internship program and continues to lecture in theology. His ThM is from Dallas Theological Seminary and his ThD from Grace Theological Seminary in Indiana. His writings include popular biblical commentaries and various articles for bible dictionaries.

Guy S. Saffold spent 14 years in administration at Trinity Western University before becoming vice president and dean of Trinity Western Seminary in 1992. He did his MDiv at Trinity Evangelical Divinity School and his EdD at Seattle University in 1987 on organizational culture, planning, and leadership. He teaches in the practical applications for ministry division. Barrie Palfreyman assumed the position of vice president and dean of the Canadian Baptist Seminary and professor of church ministries at ACTS in 1988. He has a MMin from Northwest Baptist Theological Seminary and an EdD from Seattle Pacific University. His fields are leadership, mentoring, and church administration. Vern Middleton became associate professor of missiology and church growth at Northwest in 1976 and moved with them to ACTS. He received a BD from Northwest in 1963, served as a missionary in India, and did his MTh and PhD at Fuller in church growth, writing a biographical study of Donald A. McGavran for his doctoral thesis. Kenneth H. Loudon was appointed as associate professor of counselling at Trinity Western Seminary and ACTS in 1992. His MDiv is from Fuller, as is his PhD in clinical psychology. He worked as regional staff for Inter-Varsity Christian Fellowship, as a clinic director, and in private practice prior to coming to ACTS. Two professors of psychology from the university's division of social sciences, Brian Johnson and Daniel Brinkman, also serve as adjunct facult. Johnson has a PhD in counselling psychology from the University of Alberta. Brinkman took his BA at Trinity Western University in 1981 and completed a doctorate in psychology at Western Conservative Baptist Seminary.

Most of the faculty at ACTS represent a slightly different pattern of education and appointment from the faculties of Regent and Trinity Western. Several studied not only for their earlier degrees but also for their doctorates at evangelical schools. Unlike the earlier generation of bible college teachers, however, all present faculty have doctoral degrees and all have pastoral experience. Close ties are maintained with other evangelical schools. Several members of the faculties at Trinity Western and ACTS have lectured from time to time at Regent College, though the stricter pattern of piety and formulation of beliefs required by Trinity Western University and ACTS of their faculty and students have restricted the number of Regent faculty who could reciprocate.

Smaller Institutions of Theological Studies

The patterns of faculty appointments in the smaller institutions of theological studies in BC were different. In the Roman Catholic seminary in Mission and the various bible colleges, the faculties were drawn exclusively from particular ecclesial traditions and trained largely within those traditions. The Seminary of Christ the King was entrusted to the Benedictines in 1939 as a training centre for both the secular and the religious priesthood. Its faculty of theology opened in 1951 and its faculty of arts in 1966. In 1953 the community received abbatial status under the name of Westminster Abbey. Its current statement of purpose stresses the ecclesial focus of its program:

> The goal of the Seminary Program is to form spiritual men who are well prepared for the ministerial priesthood and able to adjust to the changing needs of the Church. The Seminary gives special attention to character and spiritual formation centred on the liturgy and builds on foundations of faith and reverence laid primarily in a Christian family. The Seminary is convinced of the advantage of maturing within a community of like-minded students and of pursuing priesthood studies in a setting where Church seasons and feasts make real the mysteries of the faith and create a supportive environment for academic life.[28]

The four-year BA program focuses on those humanities that have special relevance to the study of theology. The division of religious studies within the arts faculty concentrates on the elements of Christian thought and the history of liturgy. For the MDiv degree, courses in sacred scripture, theology, moral theology, church history and patrology, canon law, and pastoral and liturgical subjects are required.

Of the 21 faculty members and lecturers in arts and theology listed in the calendar, two have doctorates: Augustine Kalberer in philosophy from the University of Toronto and Margherita Oberti from the University of British Columbia in classics. Twelve are graduates of the Seminary of Christ the King and 15 are members of the Benedictine order. Two women are on the teaching staff, one in elocution and the other in philosophy and patrology. Seventeen did advanced studies at Roman Catholic colleges or Pontifical Institutes in Rome or the United States.[29]

Columbia Bible College is jointly sponsored by the British Columbia Conference of Mennonite Brethren Churches and the Conference of Mennonite Churches in British Columbia. It was the first inter-Mennonite bible institute in North America. The college describes itself as "a training arm of the church" that seeks "to prepare students for a life of discipleship, service and ministry in the contemporary world." Its expectations of its faculty are consistent with this ecclesial purpose:

> Through deep commitment to the full and final authority of Scripture, the faculty at Columbia provides formal instruction and personal modelling of Biblical principles for daily living. A concerted effort is made to maintain an acceptable balance between being "in the world," but not "of the world," and between rigid conformity and individual liberty, in the development of responsible Christian character. Columbia is committed to the Biblical truth that the Christian life is best expressed in the context of community, not in isolation.[30]

The college offers a one-year certificate in Christian studies, a two-year diploma in Christian studies, and a four-year BRE. Each program is made up of courses in biblical studies, church ministries (including Christian education, youth and music), mission, and early childhood education. Special attention is given to training for evangelism with all ages. Credit transfer arrangements exist with Trinity Western University, the University of Waterloo, and the University of Manitoba. The BRE normally qualifies students for acceptance into graduate degree programs at Regent, ACTS, and the Mennonite seminaries in Fresno and Elkhart.[31]

Of the 19 full-time faculty listed in the catalogue, one has a PhD from Simon Fraser University, one is a doctoral candidate at Union Theological Seminary, and one has a DMin from Fuller. Sixteen have master's degrees. All 19 are graduates of Mennonite institutions of higher education in Canada or the United States. Nine studied at Columbia Bible College or its predecessors, and four at Regent. Ten taught high school prior to coming to Columbia and six were pastors in Mennonite churches. There is one woman teaching full time.

Western Pentecostal Bible College was founded by the British Columbia District of the Pentecostal Assemblies of Canada and chartered to grant degrees by the province in 1967. It exists "to help fulfil the great commission by educating students at the undergraduate level to develop full-time Christian ministers and leaders with personal spiritual maturity." The description of its philosophy of education indicates the expectations it has of its faculty:

> Christian teachers and learners ought to be outstanding examples among all other educators. But beyond the conscientious application of time and energy, and the pursuit of the best of informed procedures, there is a vital spiritual relationship. The Christian scholar also seeks to develop a responsive submission to the Holy Spirit. He recognizes that when one is pursuing God's truth, the learning process must take place in and of the Holy Spirit. This divine Spirit must be made the essential partner who expands and validates the roles of both teachers and learner.[32]

The faculty and staff of the college are drawn from the minister and membership of the Pentecostal Assemblies of Canada. The college offers a one-year discipleship program, a two-year certificate program in bible or Christian education, a three-year diploma program in pastoral theology, bible, or Christian education, a four-year BTh with majors in pastoral theology, Bible, biblical theology, or church music, and a four-year BRE.[33]

Ten full-time teaching faculty are listed in the calendar. One has a DMin from Trinity Evangelical Divinity School and one is a doctoral candidate at the University of Warwick. Four have master's degrees from Regent College, one from Trinity Evangelical, one from Wheaton, and one from Fuller. Three studied at Western Pentecostal prior to going on to further studies and returning to the faculty. Two are women. All had pastoral experience in congregations, counselling, or evangelistic programs.[34]

The broad interests and experiences of faculty members at the various institutions for the study of religion in BC have made them active members of several national and international scholarly societies and projects. These personal contacts redress the isolationism that has historically characterized the policies and practices of their institutions. In general, faculty teaching in religious studies are involved in societies connected with the Canadian Society for the Study of Religion or in the learned societies directly related to their specific disciplines. In addition, they frequently attend the societies of their disciplines at the American Academy of Religion meetings in the United States. Faculty teaching in theological studies at VST, Regent, Trinity Western University, and ACTS usually attend the same meetings. In the field of church history, faculty in all these institutions attend the meetings of the Canadian Society of Church History and the American Society of Church History. The discipline in which the most regular interchange of views takes place is biblical studies. In addition to the societies already mentioned, a symposium of faculty members teaching Hebrew and Christian scriptures at UBC, Trinity Western University, Regent, and VST meets regularly to hear and discuss papers. Faculty teaching in the evangelical schools, however, have additional networks of societies and conferences, through such organizations as the Evangelical Theological Society, the Tyndale societies, parachurch groups such as IVCF, Young Life of Canada, and Campus Crusade for Christ, and the evangelical lecture circuit. Teachers at the Seminary of Christ the King and the bible colleges move primarily within their own ecclesial networks.

As has been noted, there is some exchange of faculty in teaching roles among the major institutions under discussion. The general pattern is that UBC will hire faculty from the other institutions as lecturers in their religious studies program. The real barrier to broader exchanges is the existence of the statements of faith to which faculty are required to subscribe at Regent and Trinity Western. Most faculty teaching at UBC and VST would be unable to do this. Such institutional policies will have a significant impact on any discussions concerning the development of a doctoral program in BC.

It is among individual faculty members, then, that the institutional isolation that characterizes the study of religion in BC is breaking down. The impact of a doctoral program on this isolation is yet to be determined. The culture of civility, identified by James Davison Hunter as a feature of the contemporary academic culture, encourages faculty members with differing perspectives and commitments to be tolerant of and tolerable to each other. It remains to be determined whether this attitude of openness and acceptance is shared by the constituencies that founded and support the institutions.

Notes

1 Province of British Columbia, *An Act to Incorporate the Vancouver School of Theology, 1971*, Section 41.

2 Stewart, *Story of Union College*, 33, and Martin, "Competence Model," 128.

3 Taylor, "Report," 19-21.

4 *Senate Minutes*, Vancouver School of Theology, February 1972, np, VST Archives and *Board of Governors Minutes*, Vancouver School of Theology, 17 April 1972, 106: 9-17.

5 Vancouver School of Theology, *Faculty Handbook* (as amended 13 June, 1988), 13.

6 Martin, *Exposure and Reflection*, 1.

7 Martin, *Exposure and Reflection*, 2.

8 Martin, *Exposure and Reflection.*, 6.

9 Martin, "Vision for Mission," 72.

10 Martin, "Vision for Mission," 71.

11 The final report of the task force is found in United Church of Canada, *Educated Ministry in the United Church of Canada: Phase I, Ordained Ministry* (Toronto: Division of Ministry, Personnel, and Education, 1984).

12 This transition in Van Seters thinking can be traced through articles and editorials in *Arc*, a periodical which he co-edited for five years that was originated by Presbyterians in Montreal and subsequently published by the Faculty of Religious Studies at McGill. See *Arc*, 2, 2 (Winter 1975): 1-7; *Arc*, 5, 1 (Autumn 1977): 11-14; *Arc*, 8, 2 (Spring 1980): 22-27; *Arc*, 10, 1 (1982): 11-19; and *Arc*, 10,2 (1983): 3-6. The maturing of his social hermeneutic is found in *Preaching as a Social Act*, ed. Arthur Van Seters (Nashville: Abingdon, 1988).

13 Houston, "History and Assumptions," 2.

14 Mark A. Noll, *Between Faith and Criticism: Evangelicals, Scholarship, and the Bible in America* (San Francisco: Harper & Row, 1986), 91-121.

15 Marsden, *Reforming Fundamentalism*, 8.

16 D.W. Bebbington, *Evangelicalism in Modern Britain: A History from the 1730s to the 1980s* (London: Unwin Hyman, 1989), 259-61.

17 Noll, *Faith and Criticism*, 99-105.

18 James M. Houston, "Editorial," *Crux*, 15, 1 (March 1979): 2.

19 James D. Hunter, *Evangelicalism: The Coming Generation* (Chicago: University of Chicago Press, 1987), 184-85.

20 Craig M. Gay, "Review of *Evangelicalism:The Coming Generation*," *Crux*, 24, 2 (June 1988): 31-33.

21 Craig M. Gay, with Loren Wilkinson, Mark Noll, and James Houston, "The Uneasy Intellect of Modern Evangelicalism," *Crux*, 26, 3 (September 1990): 8-13.

22 Regent College, *Catalogue 1993-1995*, 7.

23 Regent College, *Catalogue 1993-1995*, 7.

24 This pattern was identified as characteristic of the coming generation of evangelicals by Hunter, *Evangelicalism*, 165-71.

25 See, for example, positions expressed in the faculty forum in *Crux*, 26,3 (September 1990): 8-13. Further, see the series of articles by Gordon Fee, "Issues in Evangelical Hermeneutics: Hermeneutics and the Nature of Scripture," *Crux*, 26, 2 (June 1990): 21-26, "Issues in Evangelical Hermeneutics, Part II: The Crucial Issue — Authorial Intentionality: A Proposal Regarding New Testament

Imperatives," *Crux*, 29, 3 (September 1990): 35-42, "Issues in Evangelical Hermeneutics, Part III: The Great Watershed — Intentionality & Particularity/ Eternality: I Timothy 2:8-15 as a Test Case," *Crux*, 26, 4 (December 1990): 31-37, and "Issues in Evangelical Hermeneutics, Part IV: Hermeneutics, Exegesis and the Role of Tradition," *Crux*, 27, 1 (March 1991): 12-20. Further still, see Stanley J. Grenz, *Revisioning Evangelical Theology: A Fresh Agenda for the 21st Century* (Downers Grove: Inter-Varsity Press, 1993). Grenz suggests that the identity of the evangelical coalition is to be found in a pattern of piety as much, if not more, as in a set of theological propositions. The phrase he uses to describe this evangelical identity is "an experiential piety cradled in a theology." The recent appointments and the growth in the number of courses at Regent in the area of spirituality reinforce the validity of Grenz's analysis of contemporary evangelicalism.

26 Trinity Western University, *1993/94 Academic Calendar*, 51.
27 Trinity Western University, *1993/94 Academic Calendar*, 11. On the differences between the "churchish" and "sectish" *mentalities* that characterize the doctrinal stances of Regent and Trinity Western, see Stackhouse, *Canadian Evangelicalism*, 177-204.
28 The Seminary of Christ the King, *Calendar 1991-1994*, 7.
29 The Seminary of Christ the King, *Calendar 1991-1994*, 33-35.
30 Columbia Bible College, *1992-1994 Catalogue*, 4.
31 Columbia Bible College, *1992-1994 Catalogue*, 16-17.
32 Western Pentecostal Bible College, *1992-94 Catalogue*, 30.
33 Western Pentecostal Bible College, *1992-94 Catalogue*, 6-16.
34 Western Pentecostal Bible College, *1992-94 Catalogue*, 5.

Conclusions*

The most striking irony in this survey is that the study of religion in the most secular province in Canada is structured in the most traditional ways and dominated by theological studies. Only one university department offers majors, honours, and graduate programs in religious studies, while the older nineteenth-century pattern of government-chartered Christian colleges offering bachelor's and master's degrees with specific Christian content has reappeared. Less striking, though no less significant, is the institutional isolation that characterizes the study of religion in the province. The theological and ideological tensions that unrlie the isolation have contributed to the failure of any of these institutions to develop the cooperative arrangements that would make possible a doctoral program to prepare future generations of teaching faculty and research scholars. Several concluding comments are warranted by these and other patterns identified in this survey.

The study of religion in British Columbia is dominated by theological studies to a degree unique in Canada. The Western Christian heritage, in a variety of manifestations, is well represented at both the undergraduate and graduate levels. Other religious traditions, an increasing number of whose adherents and practitioners are moving into the province, are not the subject of much serious study, either for academic analysis or religious formation, in publicly funded or recognized institutions. Religious studies cannot be said

---

* The notes to the Conclusions are on p. 110.

to be well established as a field or discipline in BC. Most of the current faculty in the UBC department received their graduate education in disciplines other than religious studies and none has participated actively in the discussions and debate concerning the nature of religious studies. Only four general courses in the study of religion are listed in the department's undergraduate offerings; one of these deals with women and religion (taught by a sessional lecturer) and another is not offered every year. The discipline of theological studies is well established, but exists in isolated pockets that seldom enter into significant dialogue with each other, especially at the institutional level. One of the original objectives of those who established the programs at UBC, VST, and Regent, namely, to foster mutual understanding and genuine dialogue among those holding different religious views, has remained an ideal rather than proceeding to a reality.

The exception to the pattern of isolation can be found among the conservative evangelical colleges in BC. Under the influence of Regent College, the fastest growing graduate school of theological studies in Canada, a new coalition of evangelicals is emerging in BC. Stan Grenz describes the movement as "a religious fellowship, a transdenominational community with complicated infrastructures or institutions, somewhat similar to a denomination but more informal." For this group, the evangelical movement rather than their particular denominations forms their primary "identity-conferring community."[1] The evidence suggests that this evangelical coalition will broaden and strengthen as Regent graduates, often following further graduate studies in respected doctoral programs throughout the English-speaking world, take faculty positions in the university and the bible colleges that serve this wing of the church in the province. The growing strength of this coalition in BC ecclesiastical life creates tensions within the older mainline denominations that sponsor VST. Significant and vocal minorities within their constituencies identify with the new evangelical coalition and look to Trinity Western University and Regent College for their higher education. Administrators and faculty at VST realize that they work within "broad church" traditions that have consciously maintained a variety of theological and devotional perspectives within their denominational fellowships. Yet it is precisely these broad church tendencies against which the evangelical movement has developed historically. To further complicate matters, the intellectual questioning and broadening going on within the evangelical movement itself is very much a part of the mix in BC. Church judicatories of the Anglican, United, Presbyterian, and Lutheran denominations have refused to date to recognize graduate degrees from Regent College or the Associated Canadian Theological Schools as sufficient for ordination to their professional ministries, but pressure to do so is growing. Just how significant this ferment within theological studies will be in breaking down the isolation of these institutions and their constituencies remains to be seen.

In the past 20 or 30 years, the departments, schools, and colleges examined in this survey have either been founded afresh or substantially rebuilt on earlier foundations. In essence, all are institutions that have seen substantial growth and expansion over those years. Student bodies, administrative structures, and faculty numbers have grown rapidly. In the case of VST, the founding generation of faculty set out to create a different kind of program for educating professional church workers prior to and following ordination or appointment. In the case of UBC's Department of Religious Studies, Regent College, and Trinity Western University, the founding faculties sought to establish programs similar to others in existence but appropriate to the BC context. The same was the case for the Roman Catholic seminary and the bible colleges. But the attention, work, and funding that went into building these institutions necessarily created a focus on the institution itself and left little energy for building inter-institutional relations across traditional theological and ideological lines, even if some interest in doing so existed. None of this growth has taken place without tensions and controversy. In some situations, such as in UBC's Department of Religious Studies in the late 1970s and early 1980s, the tensions ran high. In most situations, wise leadership and flexibility among faculties and constituencies made the tensions tolerable and, at times, creative. Since the institutions were established to serve unique needs and constituencies, little cooperation developed among them.

Financial restraints have and will continue to have a significant impact on the work of the institutions surveyed. Older institutions, such as VST, are faced with the need to do deferred maintenance on buildings that are almost seventy years old. Newer institutions, such as Regent and Trinity Western, have drawn heavily on their constituencies for capital expenses in building their facilities as well as their faculties. Government funding for eligible institutions is not increasing as quickly as costs. The costs of sustaining faculty complements and administrative structures may force decisions to cut programs and personnel as sources of funding and enrolments level out or decrease. Whether these financial realities will play a role in encouraging the institutions to look for new cooperative programs that will break down some of the isolation remains to be seen. The arena in which this seems most feasible is the development of a doctoral program using the combined resources of at least UBC, VST, and Regent. As an initial step in this direction, the UBC Senate created a new committee in 1995 with Canadian geographer Cole Harris as chair to examine the possibility of closer ties with the theological colleges affiliated with UBC in graduate work.

The records of publication among the faculties compare favourably with their colleagues across the country. This, of course, varies from person to person and from institution to institution. The lack of publication among the founding generation of faculty in UBC's Department of Religious Studies was a contributing factor in the university's brief threat to close the department, but the current generation of faculty have records that have warranted promotions in recent years. In institutions devoted to theological studies, the range of expectations in publishing, the kinds of material written, and the demands on the time of faculty in school and ecclesial matters affect the availability of time and concentration to contribute to scholarly research. Nevertheless, the output of faculty members in theological studies is significant, especially in biblical studies and church history.

One area that must receive attention as faculty are replaced or hired is the number of women in tenure-track professorial positions. In 1992, UBC had none, VST and Regent each had one teaching in Christian education, and Trinity Western had three in its Department of Arts and Religious Studies, all teaching in arts. Having women as adjunct faculty and sessional lecturers is no longer a satisfactory solution when 50 percent of the student body in these institutions is female.

The study of religion in BC will continue to be conducted in the pattern described for the foreseeable future. The various wings of the Christian tradition are well-represented, but institutes devoted to the other religions represented in the population have been discussed, some in affiliation with provincial universities. Whether these would offer degrees that paralleled those granted by the

Christian theological colleges has yet to be determined. A new initiative has been taken by the University of Victoria in establishing the Centre for Studies in Religion and Society. The Centre was established in 1991 and Harold Coward, formerly of the University of Calgary, was appointed director in 1992. The centre aims "to promote interdisciplinary dialogue through a scholarly study of religion in relation to the sciences, ethics, and other aspects of culture."[2] To achieve this end, the centre offers research fellowships for faculty at the University of Victoria, fellowships for visiting faculty, community fellowship awards, summer institutes, community seminars and lecture series, and has launched its own publications program. The centre has had much success in drawing support and interest from the community outside the university.

In a province as secular as this one, there seems to be little pressure to add religious studies departments to any of the other public provincial universities. Though the Christian community in its various forms is strong, there seems little likelihood that new institutions of theological studies will be established in times of financial restraint. Interdisciplinary and interfaith centres like that at the University of Victoria provide a new model for exploration of the role of religion in human experience, but they do not provide the means to engage in a sustained and focused study of religion at either the undergraduate or graduate level. The transfer of leadership in the study of religion in BC from the founding generation to a new generation is just beginning to take place and no clear trajectories of change have emerged. One hopes for greater intentional dialogue among the various approaches to the study of religion and the religions themselves and for the development of a doctoral program in religious/theological studies.

One clear trajectory that has emerged is not a part of the University of British Columbia, but is located at the University of Victoria. The Centre for Studies in Religion and Society is in part the result of the need for an expanded view of studies in religion. The dialogic thrust of current theologies, along with the influence of interfaith movements, has produced this Centre, the focus of which is postdoctoral research. Lectures provided at the University cover a wide range of pertinent subjects and academic interests. The interdisciplinary nature of its commitment brings together the various voices of the scholarly worlds, while not ignoring the community at large. The major challenges of global concern are addressed.

Professor Harold Coward, the first director of the Centre, obtained a BA and an MA in psychology from the University of Alberta, before doing his PhD in Indian philosophy, psychology and religion at McMaster University. A specialist in Hindu studies and a professor of history at the University of Victoria, Coward has written and edited extensively (pluralism, Jung, environmental theologies and ethics, Hindu ethics, interfaith dialogue, etc.), and has organized several world conferences and lectured widely.

Future work in the Victoria centre is expected to include an increased interchange between religion and the sciences, and between religion and the secular expressions of knowledge and opinion.

Notes

1 Grenz, *Revisioning Evangelical Theology*, 26-27.
2 Centre for Studies in Religion and Society, University of Victoria, *Annual Report 1992-1993*, 15. For the full statement of aims, see Appendix III.

Appendix 1
Courses in Religion and Cognate Subjects Offered at UBC in Other Departments and Programs

Anthropology:	332	The Analysis of Myth
	415	Religion and Society
Asian Studies:	325	History of Chinese Thought
	350	The Mythological Tradition of South Asia in Translation

(Also the appropriate canonical languages: Chinese, Sanskrit, Urdu, and Japanese)

Classics:	305	Classical Myth and Religion
English:	203	Biblical and Classical Backgrounds of English Literature
	311	Literature of the Bible
Fine Arts:	351	History of Early Chinese Art
	353	Buddhist Art of Japan
	356	Buddhist Art of Asia

Greek:	125	Introduction to New Testament Greek
Latin:	305	Medieval Latin
History:	207	Piety and Dissent in the High Middle Ages
	372	Ideas and Institutions of the Middle Ages
	413	The Reformation
	441	Anti-Semitism and Nation-Building
Italian Studies:	310	The Divine Comedy in Translation
Medieval Studies:	200	Introduction to the Middle Ages
Music:	327	Liturgical Music I
	427	Liturgical Music II
Philosophy:	317	Philosophy of Religion
	373	Medieval Philosophy: A
	383	Medieval Philosophy: B
Sociology:	463	Sociology of Religion

Appendix 2
Statements of Purpose or Faith from the Institutions of Theological Studies

Vancouver School of Theology

The mission of the Vancouver School of Theology is to be a multi-denominational community of learning on the Pacific Rim preparing clergy and lay leaders for ministry with passionate commitment to Jesus Christ for a changing church in diverse cultures.

VST Values

Compassion and equity

Integrity and excellence

Collegial and personal accountability

Biblical and theological integration

Cultural and ethnic sensitivity

Enduring relationships with aboriginal peoples

Theological reflection in the practice of ministry

An ecumenical spirit and a denominational commitment

Goals

1. To provide distinctive opportunities for the formation of effective leaders and teachers for the Church

2. To strengthen our existing relationships in keeping with changing denominational needs, partnership with aboriginal peoples, and emerging Canadian cultural diversity

3. To develop and maintain a faculty recognized for outstanding teaching and interpretation of the Christian tradition and for significant research in the disciplines of theological studies

4. To explore new partnerships especially with the theological institutions and Churches of the Pacific Rim

5. To strengthen our relationship with the University of British Columbia

6. To exercise responsible stewardship and effective communication through all the functions of the School

Regent College

We accept wholeheartedly the revelation of God given in the Scriptures of the Old and New Testaments and confession the faith therein set forth and summarized in such historic statements of the Christian church as the Apostles' Creed and the Nicene Creed. We here explicitly assert the doctrines that are regarded as crucial to the understanding and proclamation of the gospel and to practical Christian living.

1. The sovereignty and grace of God the Father, Son and Holy Spirit in creation, providence, revelation, redemption and final judgement.

2. The divine inspiration of Holy Scripture and its consequent entire trustworthiness and supreme authority in all matters of faith and conduct.

3. The universal sinfulness and guilt of human nature since the fall, bringing everyone under God's wrath and condemnation.

4. The substitutionary sacrifice of the incarnate Son of God as the sole ground of redemption from the guilt, penalty and power of sin.

5. The justification of the sinner by the grace of God through faith alone in Christ crucified and risen from the dead.

6. The illuminating, regenerating, indwelling and sanctifying work of God the Holy Spirit in the believer.

7. The unity and common priesthood of all true believers, who together form the one universal Church, the Body of which Christ is the Head.

8. The expectation of the personal, visible return of the Lord Jesus Christ.

The above points constitute the theological statement of the World Evangelical Fellowship.

Trinity Western University

As an evangelical Christian university, Trinity Western openly espouses a unifying philosophical framework to which all faculty and staff are committed without reservation. The university identifies with, and is committed to, historic orthodox Christianity as expressed by the following Statement of Faith:

We believe:

1. The Scriptures, both Old and New Testaments, to be the inspired Word of God, without error in the original writings, the complete revelation of His will for the salvation of men, and the divine and final authority for all Christian faith and life.

2. In one God, Creator of all things, infinitely perfect and eternally existing in three persons, Father, Son, and Holy Spirit.

3. That Jesus Christ is true God and true man, having been conceived of the Holy Ghost and born of the Virgin Mary. He died on the cross, a sacrifice for our sins according to the Scriptures. Further, He arose bodily from the dead, ascended into Heaven,

where at the right hand of the Majesty on High, He is now our High Priest and Advocate.

4. That the ministry of the Holy Spirit is to glorify the Lord Jesus Christ and during this age to convict men; regenerate the believing sinner; and indwell, guide, instruct and empower the believer for godly living and service.

5. That man was created in the image of God but fell into sin and is therefore lost, and only through regeneration by the Holy Spirit can salvation and spiritual life be obtained.

6. That the shed blood of Jesus Christ and His resurrection provide the only ground for justification and salvation for all who believe, and only such as receive Jesus Christ are born of the Holy Spirit and thus become children of God.

7. That water baptism and the Lord's Supper are ordinances to be observed by the Church during the present age. They are, however, not to be regarded as means of salvation.

8. That the true Church is composed of all persons who, through saving faith in Jesus Christ, have been regenerated by the Holy Spirit and are united together in the body of Christ, of which he is the Head.

9. That only those who are thus members of the true Church shall be eligible for membership in the local church.

10. That Jesus Christ is the Lord and Head of the Church, and that every local church has the right under Christ to decide and govern its own affairs.

11. In the personal, premillennial and imminent coming of our Lord Jesus Christ, and that this Blessed Hope has a vital bearing on the personal life and service of the believer.

12. In the bodily resurrection of the dead: of the believer to everlasting blessedness and joy with the Lord, and the unbeliever to judgment and everlasting conscious punishment.

Columbia Bible College

1. We believe that the whole Bible is the inspired and infallible Word of God and that it is the supreme and final authority in all matters of faith and life.

2. We believe that there is one God, eternally existing in three persons: Father, Son and Holy Spirit.

3. We believe that Jesus Christ was begotten by the Holy Spirit, born of the Virgin Mary and that He is true God and true man.

4. We believe that the Holy Spirit is a Person; that He is God, co-equal with the Father and the Son; that He convicts the world of sin, righteousness and judgment; that He regenerates and indwells the believer and is his constant teacher and guide; and that He provides the enabling power for victorious living and dedicated serving.

5. We believe that man was created in the image of God; that Adam sinned and thereby incurred for himself and for the whole human race both physical and spiritual death, the essence of which is separation from God.

6. We believe that the Lord Jesus Christ died for man's sins and that all who believe in Him have the forgiveness of sins through His blood.

7. We believe that Christ rose bodily from the dead and ascended into heaven where He is now the believer's High Priest and Advocate. He now rules over all things in heaven and on earth.

8. We believe that each individual must experience a personal regeneration, being born again of the Holy Spirit by the Word of God through personal faith in the Lord Jesus Christ, thereby becoming a child of God.

9. We believe that the church, instituted by Christ, consists of all true believers whose supreme mission in this age is to make disciples of all nations.

10. We believe that the ordinances of the church are water baptism upon personal confession of faith in Christ and the Lord's Supper whereof we partake in remembrance of Christ.

11. We believe that a life of discipleship in conformity to the teachings of Christ in the Scriptures is an essential evidence of living faith and effective service, including non-resistance to evil by carnal means, the exercise of love, and the resolute abandonment of the use of violence, including warfare. We believe that the Christian life will, of necessity, express itself in non-conformity to the world in life and conduct.

12. We believe that the imminent return of Christ from heaven will be personal and visible and that he will judge the living and the dead.

13. We believe that there will be a bodily resurrection of the just and the unjust, with a state of everlasting blessedness for the just and a state of everlasting punishment for the unjust.

Western Pentecostal Bible College

We believe ...

- the Holy Scriptures are the divinely inbreathed, infallible, inerrant and authoritative Word of God.

- that there is one God, eternally existent in the Persons of the Holy Trinity.

- in the virgin birth of the Lord Jesus Christ, His unqualified deity, His sinless humanity and perfect life, the eternal all-sufficiency of His atoning death, His bodily resurrection, His ascension to the Father's right hand, and His personal coming again at His second advent.

- that justification is a judicial act of God on the believer's behalf solely on the merits of Christ, and that regeneration by the power of the Holy Spirit is absolutely essential for personal salvation.

- in holy living, the present day reality of the baptism in the Holy Spirit according to Acts 2:4, the gifts of the Holy Spirit, and the Lord's supernatural healing of the human body.

- in Christ's Lordship of the Church, the observance of the ordinances of Christian baptism by immersion for believers and the Lord's Supper.

- in the eternal blessedness of the redeemed in heaven and the eternal doom of the unregenerate in the lake of fire.

Appendix 3
Statement of Aims of the Centre for Studies in Religion and Society

1. Purposes

The primary purpose of the Centre is to promote interdisciplinary dialogue through a scholarly study of religion in relation to the sciences, ethics, and other aspects of culture. In particular, the Centre will pursue the following goals:

a. The Centre will contribute to the University's educational objectives by opening up new avenues of scholarship. In furthering this aim, the Centre will pursue interdisciplinary research and will promote study and dialogue through lectures, seminars, conferences, publications, library acquisitions, and other appropriate activities.

b. The centre will explore connections among the world religions and religious traditions of the indigenous Native Peoples and will relate these religions and traditions, written and oral, to other aspects of culture.

c. The Centre will pursue diverse subjects not limited to any specific time, place, or culture. These might include such topics as religious currants in philosophy; religious experience in art or literature; connections between religious, philosophical, and scientific conceptions of nature; concepts of knowledge and truth in religion and science; relationships between religion and environmental issues; the role of religion in education; religious and ethical considerations in the development and application of technology; questions of theory, practice, and value in religion and science; the relationship of religious and philosophical thought to social, political, or economic behaviour; issues of authority, toleration, and freedom in religion; the role of religion in ethnic or cultural identity; and mutually formative relationships among culture, spirituality, and the sciences. The experience of women (role, status, attitudes, writings, silencing, etc.) as appropriate will be included as part of the consideration of any topic discussed.

2. Exemplifications

a. Foster critical and rigorous intellectual inquiry into values that religion, science, culture and society hold, and the way in which those values affect global well-being.

b. Explore the diversity of experiences and values, both contemporary and historical, including oral as well as literate traditions.

c. Give special attention to key issues of concern to the community at large.

d. Actively encourage the flow of knowledge between the community and the university.

e. Give preference to interdisciplinary approaches and projects.

f. Address the experience of groups which have been marginalized and excluded from defining academic issues.

g. Critically examine how knowledge is produced and how it excludes certain people and questions/issues.

Index

Series Published by Wilfrid Laurier University Press for the Canadian Corporation for Studies in Religion / Corporation Canadienne des Sciences Religieuses

Editions SR

15. *Love and the Soul: Psychological Interpretations of the Eros and Psyche Myth*
    James Gollnick
    1992 / viii + 174 pp.
16. *The Promise of Critical Theology: Essays in Honour of Charles Davis*
    Edited by Marc P. Lalonde
    1995 / xii + 146 pp.
17. *The Five Aggregates: Understanding Theravāda, Psychology and Soteriology*
    Mathieu Boisvert
    1995 / xii + 166 pp.
18. *Mysticism and Vocation*
    James R. Horne
    1995 / 152 pp. est. / FORTHCOMING

Comparative Ethics Series /
Collection d'Éthique Comparée

1. *Muslim Ethics and Modernity: A Comparative Study of the Ethical Thought
   of Sayyid Ahmad Khan and Mawlana Mawdudi*
   Sheila McDonough
   1984 / x + 130 pp. / OUT OF PRINT
2. *Methodist Education in Peru: Social Gospel, Politics, and American
   Ideological and Economic Penetration, 1888-1930*
   Rosa del Carmen Bruno-Jofré
   1988 / xiv + 223 pp.
3. *Prophets, Pastors and Public Choices: Canadian Churches and the
   Mackenzie Valley Pipeline Debate*
   Roger Hutchinson
   1992 / xiv + 142 pp.

Dissertations SR

1. *The Social Setting of the Ministry as Reflected in the Writings
   of Hermas, Clement and Ignatius*
   Harry O. Maier
   1991 / viii + 230 pp. / OUT OF PRINT
2. *Literature as Pulpit: The Christian Social Activism of Nellie L. McClung*
   Randi R. Warne
   1993 / viii + 236 pp.

Studies in Christianity and Judaism /
Études sur le christianisme et le judaïsme

1. *A Study in Anti-Gnostic Polemics: Irenaeus, Hippolytus, and Epiphanius*
   Gérard Vallée
   1981 / xii + 114 pp. / OUT OF PRINT
2. *Anti-Judaism in Early Christianity*
   Vol. 1, *Paul and the Gospels*, edited by Peter Richardson with David Granskou
   1986 / x + 232 pp.
   Vol. 2, *Separation and Polemic*
   Edited by Stephen G. Wilson
   1986 / xii + 185 pp.
3. *Society, the Sacred, and Scripture in Ancient Judaism: A Sociology of Knowledge*
   Jack N. Lightstone
   1988 / xiv + 126 pp.
4. *Law in Religious Communities in the Roman Period: The Debate Over
   Torah and Nomos in Post-Biblical Judaism and Early Christianity*
   Peter Richardson and Stephen Westerholm with A. I. Baumgarten,
   Michael Pettem and Cecilia Wassén
   1991 / x + 164 pp.

5. *Dangerous Food: 1 Corinthians 8-10 in Its Context*
   Peter D. Gooch
   1993 / xviii + 178 pp.
6. *The Rhetoric of the Babylonian Talmud, Its Social Meaning and Context*
   Jack N. Lightstone
   1994 / xiv + 317 pp.

The Study of Religion in Canada / Sciences Religieuses au Canada

1. *Religious Studies in Alberta: A State-of-the-Art Review*
   Ronald W. Neufeldt
   1983 / xiv + 145 pp.
2. *Les sciences religieuses au Québec depuis 1972*
   Louis Rousseau et Michel Despland
   1988 / 158 p.
3. *Religious Studies in Ontario: A State-of-the-Art Review*
   Harold Remus, William Closson James and Daniel Fraikin
   1992 / xviii + 422 pp.
4. *Religious Studies in Manitoba and Saskatchewan: A State-of-the-Art Review*
   John M. Badertscher, Gordon Harland and Roland E. Miller
   1993 / vi + 166 pp.
5. *The Study of Religion in British Columbia: A State-of-the-Art Review*
   Brian J. Fraser
   1995 / x + 127 pp.

SR Supplements

1. *Footnotes to a Theology: The Karl Barth Colloquium of 1972*
   Edited and Introduced by Martin Rumscheidt
   1974 / viii + 151 pp. / OUT OF PRINT
2. *Martin Heidegger's Philosophy of Religion*
   John R. Williams
   1977 / x + 190 pp. / OUT OF PRINT
3. *Mystics and Scholars: The Calgary Conference on Mysticism 1976*
   Edited by Harold Coward and Terence Penelhum
   1977 / viii + 121 pp. / OUT OF PRINT
4. *God's Intention for Man: Essays in Christian Anthropology*
   William O. Fennell
   1977 / xii + 56 pp. / OUT OF PRINT
5. *"Language" in Indian Philosophy and Religion*
   Edited and Introduced by Harold G. Coward
   1978 / x + 98 pp. / OUT OF PRINT
6. *Beyond Mysticism*
   James R. Horne
   1978 / vi + 158 pp. / OUT OF PRINT
7. *The Religious Dimension of Socrates' Thought*
   James Beckman
   1979 / xii + 276 pp. / OUT OF PRINT
8. *Native Religious Traditions*
   Edited by Earle H. Waugh and K. Dad Prithipaul
   1979 / xii + 244 pp. / OUT OF PRINT
9. *Developments in Buddhist Thought: Canadian Contributions to Buddhist Studies*
   Edited by Roy C. Amore
   1979 / iv + 196 pp.
10. *The Bodhisattva Doctrine in Buddhism*
    Edited and Introduced by Leslie S. Kawamura
    1981 / xxii + 274 pp. / OUT OF PRINT

Available from / en vente chez :

WILFRID LAURIER UNIVERSITY PRESS

Waterloo, Ontario, Canada   N2L 3C5